*Redefining*
{ beau·ti·ful }

THOMAS NELSON
*Since 1798*

NASHVILLE   DALLAS   MEXICO CITY   RIO DE JANEIRO   BEIJING

*Redefining*

# { beau·ti·ful }

[adj.]—*what God sees when God sees you*

## Jenna Lucado

### WITH MAX LUCADO

Published in Nashville, Tennessee, by Thomas Nelson. Thomas Nelson® is a registered trademark of Thomas Nelson, Inc.

Cover design by Greg Jackson
Page design by Mandi Cofer
Back cover photo by Karen James: www.karenjames.com

Thomas Nelson, Inc., titles may be purchased in bulk for educational, business, fund-raising, or sales promotional use. For information, please e-mail SpecialMarkets@ThomasNelson.com.

This story is based, in part, on true events, but certain liberties have been taken with names, places, and dates, and the characters' names have been changed in this story to protect their identification. Therefore, the persons and characters portrayed bear absolutely no resemblance whatever to the persons who were actually involved in the true events described in this book.

Unless otherwise noted, all Scripture verses taken from HOLY BIBLE: NEW INTERNATIONAL VERSION®. © 1973, 1978, 1984 by International Bible Society. Used by permission of Zondervan Publishing House. All rights reserved. Scripture quotations marked (NCV) are from New Century Version®. © 2005 by Thomas Nelson, Inc. Used by permission. All rights reserved. Scripture quotations marked (TLB) are from *The Living Bible*. © 1971. Used by permission of Tyndale House Publishers, Inc., Wheaton, Illinois 60189. All rights reserved. Scripture quotations marked (AMPLIFIED BIBLE) are from THE AMPLIFIED BIBLE: OLD TESTAMENT. © 1962, 1964 by Zondervan (used by permission); and from THE AMPLIFIED BIBLE: NEW TESTAMENT. © 1958 by the Lockman Foundation (used by permission). Scripture quotations marked (MSG) are from *The Message* by Eugene H. Peterson. © 1993, 1994, 1995, 1996, 2000. Used by permission of NavPress Publishing Group. All rights reserved. Scripture quotations marked (PHILLIPS) are from J. B. Phillips: THE NEW TESTAMENT IN MODERN ENGLISH, Revised Edition. © J. B. Phillips 1958, 1960, 1972. Used by permission of Macmillan Publishing Co., Inc. Scripture quotations marked (NLT) are from *Holy Bible*, New Living Translation. © 1996. Used by permission of Tyndale House Publishers, Inc., Wheaton, Illinois 60189. All rights reserved. Scripture quotations marked (NKJV) are from THE NEW KING JAMES VERSION. © 1982 by Thomas Nelson, Inc. Used by permission. All rights reserved.

**Library of Congress Cataloging-in-Publication Data**

Lucado, Jenna.
 Redefining beautiful : what God sees when God sees you / Jenna Lucado
with Max Lucado.
  p. cm.
  ISBN 978-1-4003-1428-7 (softcover)
  1. Teenage girls--Religious life. 2. Christian teenagers—Religious
life. 3. Self-esteem in adolescence—Religious aspects—Christianity.
I. Lucado, Max. II. Title.
 BV4531.3.L79 2009
 248.8'33—dc22

2009021703

*Printed in the United States of America*

09 10 11 12 13 RRD 6 5 4 3 2 1

*I know how to dream because you said, "I believe in you."*
*I know how to stand because you said, "I'm proud of you."*
*I know how to love because you said, "I love you."*
*And I know who I am because you said, "You are mine."*

*To my daddy on earth and to my Daddy in heaven—I knew*
*how to write this book because of you. This book is for you.*

# { contents }

# { a note from jenna }

*S*ome days I like him. Most days I hate him. But I do have to admit, he's honest. He'll always tell me if I have food in my teeth or a booger in my nose. He isn't afraid to let me know if a certain shirt is too tight or if a color doesn't complement my skin. I appreciate the honesty, but he is deceiving all the same. Deceiving because anytime he tells me, "Just get this cute shirt and feel better about yourself" or "Just lose five pounds and be forever happy," it doesn't work. I'm never good enough for him.

I try not to hang out with him too much, or else I can easily fall into his trap of discouragement—"Jenna, I see that cellulite back there. Your skin is looking pretty oily these days. Those teeth need some whitening!" I try to block out his lies that tell me I'm not good enough, that I'm not beautiful, but it's hard.

I'm sure you've met him. He tends to pop up in all sorts of places: bathrooms, cars, department stores, gyms. And I'm sure you've felt some of these same insecurities when standing in front of him.

His name?

Mirror.

Unfortunately, the mirror rarely tells me how beautiful I am. He never notices when I've helped my mom clean the kitchen or when I avoid the gossip at the lunch table. Even when I'm having a great hair day, he just notices the pimple on my chin. Because of him, sometimes I wonder if the word *beautiful* could ever describe me.

**Beautiful:** adj. 1. Having attractive qualities that give great delight or satisfaction to see, hear, think about, etc. 2. excellent of its kind. 3. particularly graceful, lovely, or pretty. . . .

Okay, so that may be the dictionary definition of *beautiful*, but let's get real. Mirror, along with his other sidekicks like TV and Magazine, seem to determine what is beautiful and what is not. We have let boys tell us whether or not we are beautiful, and sometimes we even let the popular group of girls at school define what beauty is.

Because of all of the thousands of definitions people have for beauty, we can easily get confused and struggle to see ourselves as beautiful. But the truth is, Mirror got it all wrong! He never uses the most important definition, the one that clearly states what beautiful really is:

**Beautiful:** what God sees when God sees you.

*What does beautiful mean to you? Think of someone in your life whom you consider beautiful. Why is he or she beautiful to you?*

Okay, girl, we're going to talk about all the big stuff—our looks, our clothes, and our friends. We'll share some secrets; we'll get real about our lives, dreams, parents, and God; and you *know* we're going to talk about guys!

Most importantly, we're going to talk about what *beautiful* really means, kick Mirror to the curb, and find out how really being beautiful will make your life twenty thousand times better.

*Jenna*

*chapter one*

# { weird is beautiful }

*I* 'm weird.

I really am.

If *In Style* magazine were to peg my look, I'm sure they would call it something like "Creative Casual" or "Eclectic Elegance" (although *In Style* would never feature me, because there is not much *in* to my style).

What is *your* style? Is it Disheveled Diva—waking up at the last moment, tossing on whatever fell out of the closet, throwing on a favorite pair of earrings, rushing out the door to get to school, glossing up those lips in the car, and running to first period with wild bed-head hair? Or maybe you are a Sporty Starlet—heading to class in the latest Nikes and a zip-up hoodie that matches the swoosh on your shoes, and modeling a permanent ponytail hair crease. Or are you trendy, artsy, earthy, classy, or just not interested? We all have a look. What's mine? Well . . . it's weird.

We think of fashion as our style, but c'mon, our style is so much more than that. We also accessorize with our crazy habits, silly quirks, and faithful beliefs. They are the accessories in our lives people see when they look past our clothing style and into our true style. The ones our best friends see because they know us so well. The ones God sees. But I have to be honest. Inside and out, my style is weird.

In fact, if I made a list of all my strange habits and quirky traits, I would bet a hundred bucks that my list would be so long it could wrap around the earth like a ribbon on a Christmas present. Although, let's face it, the circumference of the earth is about 25,000 miles. No one can be *that* weird . . . or can they? You judge. Here's the short version of my "Why I'm Weird" list:

1. **Guess what my number one makeup must-have is?** Go ahead. Did you guess Clinique lipstick? Bobbi Brown blush? M·A·C mascara? All very nice, but no, no, and no. The one thing I never leave home without is . . . Vaseline. Yep. Vaseline. I go through a tub of Vaseline faster than I munch a bar of Hershey chocolate. I love it! It's my all-purpose miracle ointment. I use it as a lip gloss, a makeup remover, and a lotion. If I've got some flyaway hairs, I just slick them down with a little Vaseline. For me, it is just as necessary as water and oxygen. It is one of the essential elements to my look.

2. **There is one color that is banned from my look—pink.** I really dislike pink. I don't care if *Teen Vogue* says it's "in." I don't care if *Glamour* calls it "the hot color." I won't wear it. I don't like to decorate with it. If pink were a smell, I would plug my nose. If pink were a holiday, I wouldn't celebrate it. If pink were a food, I wouldn't eat it. It's great for others, but it's not okay for me.

3.  **Instead of squealing when a cute pair of shoes goes on sale at the mall,** I'm the weirdo who actually gets excited when the king-size Snickers or Whoppers go on sale at the gas station. There's not a day that goes by when I don't pop sugary goodness into my mouth. In fact, I'm chewing on Sour Patch Kids right now because I started drooling all over my keyboard just thinking about candy. I would prefer a bag of Jelly Belly's over a Chanel crocodile-skin clutch any day.

---

**BEAUTY TIP**
*Vaseline Fixes*

*Okay, you may laugh, but I think Vaseline is very under-appreciated. Check out these cool uses of my miracle ointment:*

- *cuticle cream*

- *foot cream (Be sure to put socks on after applying; carpet and Vaseline is not a good combo!)*

- *eye moisturizer*

- *makeup remover*

- *lip gloss*

- *lotion*

- *flyaway hair controller*

*Who would've thought there'd be all this magic in one little affordable jar of petroleum jelly?*

---

The cool thing is that I'm not alone in my weirdness. Every one of us girls is weird in our own way. Just think about it. What are some of the essential elements of the look that makes you feel like *you?* Does everything have to coordinate? Do the belt, shoes, purse, skirt, and even the hair band and socks all have to match? Is *makeup* a dirty word, or is Barbie a superhero? Maybe you only wear dark-colored shirts so pit stains won't show. (Or is that just me?) How about some of those habits or traits that make you unique? Sleeping with five pillows? Watching *Full House* reruns after school? Always wearing red underwear on game days? Brushing your teeth by counting to 138? Not to 140, not to 150, but to 138.

Take a minute and list a few of your habits, likes, dislikes, personality traits, and essential elements of your unique look. In other words, what makes you weird?

*My Unique Traits:*                    *Essential Elements of My Look:*

See? You're weird too! But it's okay. Weird is beautiful!
Weirdness is what makes you . . . well . . . *you!*

## WHY WE'RE WEIRD

I used to wonder why we are the way we are. Why am I weird? Why do some people eat mayonnaise on peanut butter sandwiches? Why do some people only wear baggy jeans? And how do fashion divas become fashion divas?

Here's my conclusion: I can trace almost every weird trait and almost every unique element of my look back to the influence of someone in my life.

For example, my questionable obsession with candy comes from my mom. She always stocked candy in the house when I was growing up. She would buy it in bulk. She had a fixation for Atomic Fireballs—round, red, jaw-breaking candy that's as hot as a jalapeño. But because she only liked the hot part on the outside of the Fireball, the sweet centers were left out all over the kitchen counters. Everyone knew that if a little white ball was rolling across the floor, Mom had been sucking on her favorite candies. She would pop in one after another, filling the trash can with plastic wrappers. To this day, I don't understand why the hotness of the Fireballs didn't paralyze her taste buds for life.

And why do I hate pink? Well, in kindergarten I was sitting on the school bus next to my friend Mary. She asked me what my favorite color was. When I told her that it was pink, she made fun of me: "Pink is a stupid color! Only dummies like pink. Purple is the best color in the world." That day, my pink world shattered. I went from being a pink lover to a pink hater. No polka dot of pink or stripe of pink can be found in my closet!

Isn't it silly how such a seemingly insignificant event like that actually shaped a part of me? But those little memories, people, and events in our lives influence us more greatly than we think. They can really shape our personalities.

People can influence us in very destructive ways as well. I have a list of fears and insecurities that runs just as long as my "Why I'm Weird" list. And just as I traced my weirdness back to someone's influence in my life, I also tend to find a face at the root of my insecurities. These negative traits affect my look just as much as my quirky fashion tendencies do. After all, our look goes deeper than what's on the outside, doesn't it? It's about how we carry ourselves, how we feel others perceive us, and the disposition or attitude we display. Here are some insecurities I deal with from time to time:

1.  **I expect that people won't like me.** This is obvious in the way I try too hard to impress people. And it goes back to fourth grade when I had a crush on this boy named Steven. He was my first love—after the country singer Randy Travis, of course. I did everything I could to get Steven to like me. I tried being funny. I dressed cute. I prayed every night that he would like me. I thought I was getting somewhere—and then . . . it happened. My best friend, Amy, told me that he had asked her to be his girlfriend. I remember sitting by them in church when he gave her a ring made out of the foil wrapper that hugs a Juicy Fruit piece of gum. My heart shattered. It only took a dumb foil wrapper ring to plant the idea that I wasn't pretty enough or good enough and that I had to try even harder to make people like me. Even now, I sometimes wear myself out trying to come up with something clever or interesting to say just so others might think it's fun to hang out with me. Other times, I'll even tell myself in advance that a certain person won't like me, so that if he or she doesn't, I won't get hurt.

2.  **I am a people pleaser.** I will do anything to avoid conflict with people. Whenever I had to do a group project at school, the group project always turned into a solo project. I was always the one who volunteered to do everything—and my classmates knew it. So anytime they wanted a break from schoolwork, they all knew that they could call me and that I would assume the burden. My mouth has a hard time saying the word *no*, and I don't stand up for myself so I can avoid conflict.

3. **I have a fear of failure.** Anytime I am facing a new responsibility or opportunity, I have this overwhelming urge to run home and cry in my pillow because I am terrified that I will mess everything up. I catch myself imagining the worst rather than shooting for my dreams because I am afraid of the potential catastrophe. That kind of fear can be crippling.

4. **I used to struggle with my appearance.** At times, I still do. The insecurities started in middle school when every girl was getting boobs except me. I was what my mom likes to call a "late bloomer." Well, I was sick of the long winter! I was the only one in my circle of friends who didn't have anything blooming on her chest. I remember finding corners in the locker room so that no one could see my training bra. When I got older, I focused on my flaws all the time, thinking that I wasn't skinny enough or my face wasn't clear enough. I was never content with my clothes. I was insecure about my look, and I chose to focus on the negative parts of my physical appearance instead of finding the good.

What about you? What are some of your own struggles and fears? What insecurities do you battle?

*I feel insecure about . . .*

*Redefining* { beau · ti · ful }

Where does this stuff come from? Well, for me, a lot of the worries and fears I just shared go back to a negative influence that someone had on my life.

For example: My middle-school piano teacher was not a self-esteem booster.

Whenever I looked at him, I saw Beethoven—a brilliant musician in dire need of anger-management counseling. Even his hair was wild like Beethoven's. I cried before every piano lesson and begged my mom not to make me go. My fingers would hover over the keys, trembling like a bowl of JELL-O in the hands of a two-year-old. I knew if I messed up, my teacher would yell and bang his fingers on the keys I missed. During the few years I spent with him, my fear of failure grew and grew.

Later on, whether a teacher glared at me for an incorrect answer or I missed the last serve in a volleyball game, the disappointed faces of those around me stirred up that fear of failure.

So often I wish that what people say or think about me would not affect me. I long to feel so loved, so complete, and so beautiful that no one's hurtful words could bring me down. I long for a confidence in who I am—a confidence that is strong enough to stand up against the stones that people throw at me, and the ones I think they'd *like* to throw at me. Do you ever want that?

When I went to college, I met a girl who radiated confidence. Her name was Melanie. She loved everyone, and everyone loved her. She was a natural leader who had a lot of friends. Every time I ran into her, she took time out of her day to listen to my problems, encourage me, and make me smile. She never wore the trendiest clothes. Come to think of it, I never even saw her put on makeup. But she had a look that said, "I am comfortable with who I am. I am secure and confident." That confidence was a beauty I hadn't seen in teens my age. It wasn't the kind of look found in magazines or on the Style Network, but it was a look I wanted.

## GETTING THE LOOK

How can we get Melanie's look? How can we feel so secure in our skin that our slouching shoulders straighten, our darting eyes focus, our fears disappear, and our insecurities about boys and friends give way to unwavering confidence?

I'd like to add Melanie's secret fashion accessories to my look. But before I can get what she has, I've got to make a little room. Something has to go. I go through phases when I am bored with all of my clothes. I get sick of my look. Anytime that happens, I go on a cleaning spree. I start cleaning out every centimeter of my closet. I toss out old shirts, shoes, and purses that remind me of my old look.

You and I are about to go on a cleaning spree, but I'm not

talking about cleaning out a closet. And you might be surprised at how this new look can influence everything in your life. Plus, it's free! We're going to clean up our hearts a little. Let's get rid of all the bad stuff that prevents us from having a fresh look—a look that radiates joy, that sparkles with confidence, and that says, "I am beautifully and wonderfully made."

It's time to redefine *beautiful*.

*chapter two*

# { forgetting
# deodorant }

*I* always forget to put on deodorant. The worst part about those days is the moment I realize I am not wearing deodorant. I immediately get self-conscious. The nerves trigger the sweat glands, and the floodgates open. Feeling the pit stains begin to form adds another layer of self-consciousness and another layer of sweat, and the sweaty cycle continues.

The other day I decided to run some errands at the mall. I was a mess. I had rushed out of the house without brushing my teeth. Half of my hair was in a ponytail. The other half? Well, I have no idea what the other half was doing. I just know it was in my face. Then, halfway through my shopping, I looked down and noticed something that made my frumpiness even worse: I was still wearing my house slippers!

*Two things I've learned: one, how to laugh at myself in awkward moments, and, two, how to avoid forgetting things by tricking myself into remembering—such as placing an extra deodorant in my purse or backpack.*

*So, to curb a few potentially humiliating experiences, grab a cute makeup bag and stash a few essentials like deodorant, tampons, and maybe some hair bands for that spur-of-the-moment ponytail. Keep it in your car, backpack, or locker. (And if anyone has a tip on remembering shoes . . . let me know!)*

When my friends and I discuss awkward moments like this, few can top the things I've done. Can you?

*What's the most awkward moment you've ever had because of something you've forgotten?*

## Fashion *Un*essentials

Fashion magazine articles dramatize the basic "must-haves" for this season's look. Don't even think about leaving the house without the latest clutch or those new metallic flats, and why bother wearing those without the latest and greatest foundation, powder, and eye shadow? It's sell, sell, sell. And the goal, of course, is for us to buy, buy, buy.

Hopefully, in our hearts we know we will be okay without all of the latest trendy accessories. The latest fads often just aren't as crucial as they may seem. Really, give me a pair of shoes and some deodorant, and I'll be just fine.

Beyond pit-stain patrol and footwear, there are some *real* "must-haves" that God considers essential to a girl's look—and I'm not talking about *fashion* accessories. Real beauty has little to do with those things. Have you ever met someone who dresses outrageously, but does so with such confidence that her style becomes cool? It wasn't the clothes she wore that made her attractive, was it? Our true look is based on who we are on the inside. And, believe it or not, how our hearts are on the inside determines the way we look on the outside. Think about it. Have you ever seen anyone so stressed or upset that it changed how she looked on the outside? Have you ever been that stressed? Stiff facial expressions, a harsh tone of voice, or serious impatience with others are just a few examples. But whatever the reaction, the result is the same: you are not *you*!

No matter how beautiful we've made up our outside, if we don't have the right inside accessories, we won't look great. So, where do we get those accessories? And what are they? What is it that we really need?

*Write down the accessories you think you need in your life:*

_____

_____

_____

_____

_____

_____

_____

Sometimes we don't really know what we need, and sometimes we think we need things we really don't . . .

## Less Is More

When I was a freshman in high school, I blamed God for forgetting to give me an important accessory that all my friends had—a boyfriend. I thought it was unfair that they all had a guy telling them that they were beautiful. I thought it was unfair that they had someone to dress up for at school. And I especially thought it was unfair that they had a name to doodle all over their notebooks. I wanted a name that I could write in bubble letters that would fill in the empty margins I had on all my spirals:

I ♡ _____.

I pleaded with God for a boyfriend. Finally, toward the end of the year, I found one! He was cute, funny, nice, cute, tall, athletic—and did I mention cute?

After a few months of dating, butterflies, and holding hands, the worst thing happened: he and his family moved. They moved! My first-ever, way-cute, popular, funny boyfriend left Texas for New Jersey! I was so mad at God! What was he thinking? I felt like he had ripped out a part of me. He had taken away an essential part of my look, a piece of me!

Looking back, I can see exactly why God wanted to separate me from my boyfriend. At that point in my life, I didn't care so much about drawing physical boundaries. My friends would brag about how far they went with their boyfriends, so I wanted to do the same. I grew up knowing that I was supposed to remain a virgin until I was married, but I thought everything but sex was acceptable. Well, God ended up saving me from a lot of heartache. I know that if my boyfriend had remained in town, I would have given him a huge part of my heart that was not meant for him.

Too often we think we need a certain something that God hasn't given us when, in reality, he is protecting us from something that would spoil us. It's a principle in the fashion world: sometimes less is more. In this case, less boyfriend was exactly what my look needed.

*What are some things you used to really want, but now looking back you realize God spared you by not giving them to you?*

_____

_____

_____

_____

So, my boyfriend was an unnecessary accessory.

However, sometimes people really are missing things they need—a loving parent; an encouraging mentor; or a really close friend, someone to stay up with all night, watching movies and spilling secrets. Sometimes we girls hate looking in the mirror;

we think we're ugly because there's no one around to tell us we are beautiful. Or maybe we don't get invited out on the weekends like others do; we go through periods where we feel lonely or left out. It's especially important during those times that we're seeking the right accessories. So what are they? Well, here's a list of my top eight Life Accessories:

## LIFE ACCESSORIES

- *Security—trusting that no matter what, we have a God who loves us*

- *Identity—in knowing who we are and whose we are*

- *Value—knowing we are treasured*

- *Love—knowing God's love for us so we can love others*

- *Self-control—for making good decisions*

- *Peace—in believing God is in control*

- *Joy—in knowing the Source of all joy*

- *Contentment—in who God made you to be*

I've found that wearing these accessories (especially all at once) makes people beautiful inside and out! People who are clothed in these eight essentials are my favorite people to be around.

Unfortunately, we can't buy these essentials at Neiman Marcus, and Target doesn't carry any discount versions. Bummer, I know. In fact, sometimes there are people and things in our lives that do more to keep these essential heart accessories away from us. And sometimes we are *missing* elements in our lives that hinder us from having them.

If you have ever felt like you're missing some of these life accessories, you are not alone.

*Which of these accessories do you wear on a regular basis? And which do you wish you had? Are there people in your life who have influenced whether or not you wear some of these life accessories?*

*Redefining* { beau·ti·ful }

One person who made a huge impact in my life was my dad. Because he wears socks with sandals, he's not the first person I ask fashion questions to . . . in fact, I never ask him fashion questions. But when it comes to accessorizing my *life* . . . he has taught me a lot! He has challenged and shaped me in so many ways. Dad reminds me I'm beautiful, inside and out, and he has taught me how to find and have real beauty.

We're going to spend some time with my dad, Max, in the chapters to come.

*chapter three*

# { backdoor
# sunburn }

*D*ad! Stop!" Those two words sum up a lot of my middle and high school careers. Whether it was trying to put an end to his goofy dance moves or his loud singing in public, I was his nudge in the side or his tug on the shirt to halt all embarrassing activities.

Eventually I grew to love all of his "embarrassing" quirks and grew a deep gratitude for his influence in my life. But I never dreamed just how important every dad can be.

The connection between a father's high involvement in his child's academic career "is associated with higher grades in high school."[1] In fact, it is reported that "half of all children with highly involved fathers in two-parent families reported getting mostly A's through twelfth grade, compared with 31.7 percent of children who come from families without an active father."[2]

Is there a certain store where you buy the majority of your clothes? Sometimes my friends tell me, "You are such a Forever 21 girl!" If someone were to peg where you get your style, what store would it be? Maybe you are a GAP girl. You could be thinking, *I am a thrift store kind of girl*, or are you sitting there thinking, *Hand-me-downs make up my style?* A lot of times there is a primary store we stock our closets from. Dads are kinda like that primary store. A lot of our style comes from their influence and our relationships with them. I'm not talking just about the way we look on the outside (although dads can affect our physical appearance), but dads help define elements that make up who we are, like how we look at ourselves and everyone around us. In other words, they affect our *out*look. And our outlook gives us a certain perspective on every aspect of life and every person we meet: it either adds a dull, cloudy gray to our world, or it brightens the colors around us, making everything more beautiful. It's kind of crazy, but his love can completely transform the way we look.

Internationally known psychologist Dr. Kevin Leman has done a lot of research on this daddy/daughter stuff. He said, "The [most important] ingredient in any woman's life is her relationship with her father."[3]

That's because God designed a father's love to be an essential building block in a girl's heart. But if dads are key to shaping the women we become, we have a major problem: there are lots of girls out there without dads—and, unfortunately, many girls who do have dads don't have good ones.

Consider this: "If you were to take a map of America and draw a line down the middle of the country and, on one side, put all the children who were going to grow up between birth and age eighteen living with their father, and on the other side, all of the children who will not have that experience, there would be about the same number of children on each side of the line."[4]

Maybe you've never met your dad, or he passed away, or he

moved out. Or maybe he lives in the same house with you, but you ache to know that he loves you. And because of this, you really struggle with a lot of insecurities.

Perhaps you fall on the other side of the line, and you have a great relationship with your dad.

For good or for bad, dads profoundly affect the lives of their daughters . . .

## Maggie

Maggie is sixteen years old. When I asked her about her dad, she just laughed an awkward chuckle. "I don't know. I don't really care. I guess I love him, but I don't really think about him that much."

Her sad eyes avoided mine; I could see the hurt there. Shifting from one foot to the other and kicking the dirt, she didn't know what else to say.

I prodded a little more. "Are your parents still living together?"

"No."

"How long did he live with you?"

"He left when I was pretty young. I still remember a time when I went to visit him. I was probably like seven years old or something. He told me that I had gotten fat since the last time he saw me." She let out a nervous laugh.

## Mallory

Mallory is fifteen years old. She lives with her stepdad. She said that she couldn't repeat some of the names he calls her. They are too dirty. She did tell me that he calls her stupid, ugly, and dumb—and she started crying. That's when I looked down at her arms and saw the scars.

"One day I just started cutting myself," she said through tears.

"Why?" I asked.

"My whole life, my stepdad has yelled at me for crying. We don't cry in my house." Turns out, cutting is a way for Mallory to feel pain that she isn't allowed to feel at home.

Girls remember the times their dads spent time with them—if dad was there to shake their date's hand, kiss them good-bye on prom night, or help them with homework . . . and they remember if he wasn't there.

## BOILED NOODLES AND REVLON LIPSTICK

I love going to the lake in the summer. My family and I used to take the boat out from sunup to sundown. Dad would pull us on water skis and whip us around on the tube until our arms were as limp as boiled noodles. One of my favorite parts about going to the lake was getting that long-awaited (and much needed) tan. I loved it when the sun was high and the clouds were nowhere to be found. My white, almost transparent, skin would soak in the sun like a sponge soaks up water.

One morning *I* was ready to play on the lake, but the *sun* wasn't. It was hiding behind a thick blanket of clouds. I tried talking it into coming out for the day, but it completely ignored me. So rude! Since the sun refused me, I refused the sunscreen. After all, there was no sun to screen, right? Wow, was I wrong!

The next morning I was practically drowning in my own drool, sleeping like a bear in the winter, until . . . I rolled over. Usually rolling over isn't a big deal, right? Not that morning. I screamed so loudly you would have thought someone had stabbed me with a fork! My skin was as crispy as fried chicken fingers and as red as Revlon lipstick. But how could that be? The sun hadn't even been seen the day before!

Well, just because I couldn't see the sun didn't mean it couldn't see me. Just because I didn't feel the UV rays destroying my defenseless skin didn't mean they wouldn't mercilessly burn me.

## BEAUTY TIP
### Screen Your Skin

*Whenever Mom told us to wear sunscreen, I would always say: "Mom, I'm not going to wear sunscreen because I'm building my base tan for the summer." Man, was I wrong! I have learned the hard way that there is never an excuse to let your skin burn. Aside from preventing skin cancer, sunscreen also protects us from aging prematurely.*

*So be smart. Wear sunscreen not only when you play in the sun, but try a moisturizer or foundation with sunscreen in it for daily use.*

Just like an unforeseen burn from the sun's rays on a cloudy day, unexpected side effects from our relationships with our dads can sneak up on us when we think we are safe. Just when we think we don't have any emotional scars, just when we think Dad didn't affect the way we are now . . . *BAM!* Something happens. Shawn, for instance, realizes her stomach gets upset anytime she is alone with a man because the alone times with her dad led to abuse. Lauren realizes she doesn't respect authority because her dad gives her everything she wants. Katy realizes that she is afraid of marriage and intimacy because she sees her parents' marriage falling apart. Lesley doesn't feel happy unless she has a boyfriend, because she craves the male attention she's not getting at home. Kylie doesn't think she is pretty enough, smart enough, or good enough because she has never been pretty enough, smart enough, or good enough for her dad.

*Can you relate to one of these girls?*

_____

_____

_____

Hopefully your dad has influenced the way you look at yourself and the way you look at others in a positive way. I was fortunate to have a healthy relationship with my dad when I was growing up. He was really good about telling me how proud he was of me. Because of that, he gave me one of my must-have accessories I mentioned earlier: self-confidence. But I took it for granted. I never realized how much I depended on my dad's encouragement

*Redefining* { beau · ti · ful }

until I left for college. After I left home, I started feeling more insecure about myself. I was more intimidated in the classroom, and I suffered from a lot of anxiety about making friends. It took me a while to realize that I was stressed because I wasn't living with my biggest fan anymore! The girls in the dorm weren't going to come up to me and say, "Jenna, I am so proud of you!" the way my dad did. I had never noticed how much my dad's words affected my heart. That truth snuck through the back door like a sunburn on a cloudy day. I realized how much my relationship with him really defined a lot of who I was. It impacted how I felt and how I looked at myself.

You may or may not see it now, but three big areas of life are significantly influenced by a daughter's relationship with her dad:

*the way she looks at herself*

*the way she looks at others*

*the way she looks at God*

1. **Looking at Yourself**

A lot of doctors and researchers say that having interactive, healthy relationships with their dads improves the way girls look at themselves:

"Involved and caring fathers are important for the psychological well-being of their children, including happiness, life satisfaction, and less distress."[5]

"Through loving and being loved by their fathers, girls learn that they are love-worthy."[6]

"A father's love defines a daughter's femininity, shapes her character, affirms her identity, and validates her."[7]

2. **Looking at Others**

Dads also shape the way girls look at others and have relationships with them. Check this out:

"Girls learn from their fathers how to relate to men. They learn from their fathers about heterosexual trust, intimacy, and difference."[8]

Dads also model what a marriage relationship looks like, so if a girl has watched her parents' relationship crumble, her example of marriage is tainted. "Parental divorce increased the likelihood that a daughter's first marriage would end in divorce by 114 percent."[9]

"Adolescents from broken homes were more likely to show a higher level of distrust of other people."[10]

"Children who feel a closeness to their father are . . . 75 percent less likely to have a teen birth."[11]

3. **Looking at God**

This may be no surprise, but the way we look at God is greatly influenced by our dads:

"God intended that a father's love and care would mirror his own tender affection. . . . But when our relationships with our earthly fathers result in brokenness, that reflection of his love becomes warped or even shattered."[12]

"Many young daughters shape their view of God largely by how they view their fathers. Even as they mature and begin to see more of their father's faults . . . they're going to pick up on how this man relates to the Creator of the universe."[13]

Having a great dad can be a major contributor to growing up with a healthy view of ourselves, others, and God. But even if we have the best dad in the world and he gives pounds of encouragement and gallons of love, we will still struggle with fears and insecurities. We may measure our worth by our popularity, or we may desperately want to be liked by a certain guy. Even if Dad is great, at times we still find ourselves wanting to be a little thinner, a little smarter, a little more athletic, or . . . fill in the blank. Whether your dad is wonderful, terrible, or somewhere in between, remember that no earthly dad is perfect enough to flawlessly complete our look. Dads may be a primary source of our style, but they are not perfect enough to help us be totally confident; to help us always have healthy relationships; or even to help us always see God in the right way. Take it from one who knows.

## ME AND DAD

Let me tell you a little about my relationship with my dad.

My dad has soared in his career, loved and served thousands of people, and accomplished his highest goals, but I brag about him for one thing and one thing only: he is an out-of-this-world dad. He's always been a faithful, involved, loving dad. I know how to love myself because he loves me. I watched him love other people, so I learned to love others. And I watched him love God, which taught me how to love God.

But just because I grew up with a good dad doesn't mean there haven't been times when I didn't climb some mountains of self-doubt, experience spiritual confusion, and settle for superficial friendships.

My dad's love was not strong enough to keep me from kneeling in front of the toilet and trying to make myself throw up. He couldn't prevent me from thinking I was fat . . . especially on one Easter Sunday. I had just spent the afternoon filling my stomach with green bean casserole, buttered rolls, macaroni and cheese, cookies—a potluck of calories. After I got home, I felt guilty, and I was angry with myself. Why had I done that? Summer was around the corner. I had been on a strict diet to look good in my summer swimsuit. I thought that throwing up would serve as punishment to myself and relieve the guilt I felt. But what was the real problem here?

- The real problem was that I believed the world's definition of beauty—the lie that we aren't beautiful unless we wear a size 0.
- The real problem was that I cared more about my appearance than about my heart, and I was willing to harm myself physically, emotionally, and spiritually just to be thin.
- The real problem was that I didn't feel good enough. I didn't feel pretty enough.

I know my dad loves me. He calls me "Beautiful" all the time, but I still turned to magazine covers for my definition of beauty. I still ached for other people's approval.

## LIFE ACCESSORY
*Security—trusting no matter what, we have a God who loves us*

*I made a big mistake by trying to find all my security in my dad's love and in other people's approval. Not possible. Ever. When I did that, I was constantly insecure and unsatisfied with myself.*

*I really started to feel secure when I started to focus on God. People will always make mistakes, have biased opinions, or just not be there all of the time. But God is the one who will never leave, the home that will never be destroyed, and the family that won't be broken.*

*Next time you feel insecure, do what Hebrews 12:2 says: "Fix [your] eyes on Jesus." Taking your eyes off of yourself and turning them onto the One who loves you and helps you know you are beautiful.*

### Why It's Beautiful
*Secure people are usually pretty calm and relaxed, and this shows on their faces and in their manner. They don't brag or put down other people. Why should they? They're comfortable with who they are. Secure people relate well with others because they don't have ulterior motives.*

*chapter four*

# { quiz: what's your style and why? }

*L*et's take a little Life Accessory quiz to see what part of your heart needs a little makeover. Our beauty is often seen (or not!) in the way we relate to others and the way we feel about ourselves. Let's find out which Life Accessories we're wearing and which we're lacking, starting with boys.

## RELATIONSHIPS WITH BOYS

1. You are shopping at the mall. While you are leaving the food court, you see a cute boy, and you . . .

   a. Make a mad dash to introduce yourself, and before you're finished flirting, you make sure he has your number.

   b. Immediately turn the other way and think, *There's no way he would ever even look at a girl like me.*

c.    Grumble under your breath, "He's probably just like every other good-looking guy—a big jerk."

d.    Whisper a little prayer that he will notice you, but hang back, hoping that he will make the first move. No way would you approach him!

Now let's take that quiz a step further and analyze the response. Read the following questions, and then take some time to think about the answer you circled in this section.

**If you answered a:**

*Do you basically have no fear when it comes to approaching guys? If so, why?*

---

---

---

---

---

*Have you used your fearless tactics? If so, how have those*
*relationships turned out?*

_____

_____

_____

_____

_____

## If you answered b:

*Why do you get so nervous talking to boys?*

_____

_____

_____

_____

_____

*Have you ever had an embarrassing experience with a guy who hurt you? Describe it.*

_____

_____

_____

_____

_____

**If you answered c:**

*Do you have a cynical view of men? Explain—and if so, why?*

_____

_____

_____

_____

Redefining {beau·ti·ful}

*What guys have let you down?*

_____

_____

_____

_____

_____

_____

**If you answered d:**

*Why do you believe the guy should approach the girl?*

_____

_____

_____

_____

_____

*What examples of good men have you had in your life? Have they set a high standard for you? If so, how?*

_____

_____

_____

_____

_____

### RELATIONSHIPS WITH FRIENDS

1.  One of your best friends had a party at her house and didn't invite you. You decide to . . .

    a.  March up to her in the cafeteria and, in front of everyone, demand to know why you weren't invited.

    b.  Avoid the situation. Hating confrontation, you pretend nothing is wrong.

    c.  Stop talking to her. Girls are drama. Who needs girlfriends anyway?

d.   Find a time when it's just the two of you and tell her that not being invited hurt your feelings. Then ask what is going on that made her not want to include you.

**If you answered a:**

*Do you like confronting friends when they have hurt you? If so, what ways are there to confront that are especially helpful or even healing? What ways are not?*

_____

_____

_____

_____

*Do you like to be in a certain group at school? What makes you want to be part of that particular group?*

_____

_____

_____

**If you answered b:**

*Is it hard to confront friends? Why or why not?*

_____

_____

_____

_____

*What is your role in your group of friends? Are you the leader, the follower, the listener, or . . . ? If so, why?*

_____

_____

_____

_____

_____

*Redefining* {beau · ti · ful}

**If you answered c:**

*Have you been hurt by a friend before? If so, how did he or she hurt you?*

_____

_____

_____

_____

_____

*What friend, if any, has been a real encourager, a good listener, and a trusted soul mate? What made her different?*

_____

_____

_____

_____

_____

_____

**If you answered d:**

*Is it easier for you than it is for others to bring up tough issues with friends? How did you learn to handle situations this way?*

_____

_____

_____

_____

*What examples have you seen that have helped you learn to relate to your friends?*

_____

_____

_____

_____

Redefining { beau · ti · ful }

## RELATIONSHIPS WITH PEOPLE IN CHARGE AND YOUR FAMILY

1.  Two girls in geometry class are passing notes. When one of them asks you to pass a note to her friend, the teacher thinks you are the note-passing culprit and gives you Saturday-morning detention. You . . .

    a.  Snap back at the teacher, telling her she had better check her facts before punishing an innocent bystander.

    b.  Get tears in your eyes. Pray that everyone will stop looking at you and just accept the punishment.

    c.  Laugh and sit through the rest of the period with a smirk on your face, thinking, *It's not even worth explaining because teachers don't get it, and they're always hassling me . . . anyway, I'm not gonna show up Saturday morning.*

    d.  Go up to the teacher after class, ask to talk to her, explain the situation, and apologize for getting in the middle of it all.

2.  You arrive home excited because your dad has promised to take you to the mall to pick out a homecoming dress. But instead of waiting at the door with the keys, he is standing at the door with a broom. He asks you to help clean the house for some company that is coming into town that evening. You . . .

    a.  Begin to cry and scream, "But you promised me a homecoming dress! You lied to me! What am I going to wear? My swimsuit?"

b.   Nod and begin to clean without asking questions, but thinking, *I probably shouldn't go to homecoming anyway. I don't know the first thing about dancing.*

c.   Smirk and blurt out, "Thanks a lot, Dad. And just how many promises are you going to break in this lifetime?"

d.   Begin to sweep, then take a deep breath and respectfully remind Dad about the homecoming dress. You ask if the shopping trip can still happen once the house is clean.

**If you answered *a*'s:**

*Why do teachers get on your nerves?*

_____

_____

_____

_____

_____

_____

*Redefining* {beau·ti·ful}

*Is your dad strict or lax about rules? How do you generally respond to his orders?*

_____

_____

_____

_____

_____

**If you answered *b*'s:**

*Do you tend to simply accept unfair situations and take the blame? If so, why?*

_____

_____

_____

_____

_____

*Does your dad tell you how great you are, or does he point out your flaws more often than he says positive things?*

_____

_____

_____

_____

_____

**If you answered *c*'s:**

*Is it hard to think that teachers are on your side? If so, why? What are your relationships with your teachers and the principals at school like?*

_____

_____

_____

_____

_____

*Redefining* { beau · ti · ful }

*When, if ever, has your dad disappointed you?*

_____

_____

_____

_____

_____

**If you answered _d_'s:**

*Why is it easy to have good relationships with your teachers?*

_____

_____

_____

_____

_____

*What gives you confidence in the fact that your dad loves you and wants to come through for you?*

-----------------------------------------

-----------------------------------------

-----------------------------------------

-----------------------------------------

-----------------------------------------

### RELATIONSHIP WITH YOURSELF:

1.  Varsity soccer tryouts were this week, but you didn't make it. Instead, you're put on the JV team. You . . .

    a.  Throw a fit, march up to the coach, and give him a piece of your mind; then join a club team. *Coach will be sorry he didn't choose me,* you think.

    b.  Go home and decide to never try out again for anything. After all, not going out for anything will protect you from getting your hopes up ever again.

*Redefining* { beau • ti • ful }

c.  Say, "whatever," and walk out. Forget JV! There is no way you would play on such a dumb team with a dumb coach who doesn't care about you—just like everyone else.

d.  Decide to try your best on JV. It can only make you a better player. Maybe next year will be your year!

**If you answered a:**

*Do you find yourself getting what you want no matter what? If so, do you think that's a good thing?*

_____

_____

_____

_____

_____

_____

**If you answered b:**

*Do you assume the worst will happen to you? If so, why? Do you allow yourself to dream big?*

_____

_____

_____

_____

_____

**If you answered c:**

*Have you ever had anyone tell you how talented you are? Do you believe in yourself?*

_____

_____

_____

_____

Redefining { beau • ti • ful }

**If you answered d:**

*Do you tend to think more positive thoughts about yourself or negative thoughts? Why?*

_____

_____

_____

_____

So why did I ask you why you chose your answers? Well, I wanted you to really search your heart and think about why you do what you do. We talked earlier about how dads influence our style—how we act and who we become. In fact, I bet your dad influenced a lot of the answers you put on your quiz about boys, friends, other people, and yourself without you even realizing it. Let's dive a little deeper into what that means.

Dr. Meg Meeker has been a physician for more than twenty years, and she wrote *Strong Fathers, Strong Daughters*—a book about the influence a father has on his daughters. She wrote it because of the number of teenage girls who walk into her office and are struggling through life because of an absent father. She says, "You watch to see if he lies or tells the truth, stays faithful to your mother, works hard and speaks out against wrong behavior in the workplace as well as at home. Ninety percent of the influence a father has over his daughter's moral values comes from his behavior."[1]

## Marry Me in Miami

I love listening to my parents tell me about how they fell in love.

They had graduated from the same college in a small West Texas town, and each had randomly moved to Miami, Florida. Dad was a minister, and Mom taught at the school affiliated with the church where he worked. It's funny to hear their different perspectives. If you ask Dad when he fell in love, he will tell you that it was the first night he laid eyes on Mom. But if you ask Mom when she fell in love, she will pause slightly. "Hmmm. It took me a little while. I just thought he was funny at first, and I wanted to be his friend. Eventually, the friendship evolved into love." Dad never gave up. Having immediately fallen in love, he pursued my mom until she walked down the aisle at the same small Miami church where their relationship began.

Dad hasn't stopped pursuing her since. Hearing their history and watching my dad love my mom taught me the importance of the guy chasing the girl. I didn't want to be a girl who called a boy before he called me. I knew that I wanted a guy who had confidence, and a truly confident guy will approach the girl before she approaches him. After all, which is harder: for a guy to look you in the eyes and ask you out on a date, or for him to shoot you a text saying, "Wanna hang out?" Looking someone in the eyes is a lot harder than looking at a cell phone keypad. Each of us deserves a man who isn't going to take the easy way out. So I wasn't a girl who initiated the flirting, because my dad taught me what my role was. I know that I deserve to be pursued, and so do you!

But without a loving dad, you may be a little confused about how to interact with boys. Heidi tends to wear the pants in her romantic relationships, but that often leaves her feeling confused and insecure. Jen doesn't have high expectations about who will date her, so she settles for boys who push her to compromise her morals or who treat her badly. Nikki doesn't even want to talk to boys because the primary man in her life—her dad—hurt her, so she thinks all men will hurt her. Christy's low self-esteem makes her think she doesn't deserve a good guy. You may have never thought about this before—that your dad's example clearly impacts the way you approach boys and the way you handle relationships with them.

## HOW YOU LOOK AT FRIENDS

### A NOTE FROM MAX

*Friendliness—hospitality—is a virtue that brings as much joy to the giver as to the receiver.*

*When you extend hospitality to others, you're not trying to impress people, you're trying to reflect God to them.*[2]

What kinds of girls and guys do you hang out with? Do they build you up or tear you down? Jordan, for example, has accessory friends: they don't necessarily encourage her or discourage her, but Jordan sure looks popular as she and her friends walk down the school hallway together, with arms interlocked and steps synchronized. Amanda keeps friends at arm's length, because it's easier and safer not to get too attached to them. Kate likes cynical friends, because they fit with the depression she dwells in. Finally, Maddie has close, kindred soul-mate friends— people who challenge her and can be challenged by her.

Now think about your role in your friendships? Are you a follower or a leader? Are you the funny one, the gossip, the advice giver, the drama queen, the fighter, or something else?

Dads affect how we look at our friendships and how we interact with our friends. I have a very vivid memory of my dad teaching me how to treat friends:

## Gossip Girl

I was riding in my mom's station wagon when I was in middle school. There were two rows of seats in the back, and I sat next to my friend in the middle, while my sister and her friend sat behind us. I leaned over and told my friend that I thought my sister's friend was fat. Right as I said it, the car went quiet. I froze, and my heart immediately sank. *Did she hear me? Should I say something?* I decided to shrug it off. But the more I tried to shrug, the more I felt a tug. I had to relieve my conscience.

Later that day I told my dad what I had said. He gently explained that it is good to never go to bed with problems unresolved. The faster you apologize or correct the situation, the better you will feel. He encouraged me to call her and clear my conscience. The ironic part of the story is that I ended up confessing what I had said, but she had never even heard me! I ended up ratting myself out! Even so, it felt good to be honest and open. Dad taught me to be a good friend to others, even when it's not easy.

## BEAUTY TIP
### Bedtime Routines

*Resolving issues hanging over us before going to bed is a great way to prepare for a good night's rest. Here are some other great nighttime routines your body will appreciate:*

- *Engage in calming activities during the hour or so before bed. Give your body a chance to start winding down.*

- *Go to bed as early as possible. This can be tough (at least it is for me), but some scientists say that one hour of sleep before midnight is worth two after midnight.*

- *Leave all your worries with God. Looming burdens keep you awake and can cause fitful dreams, and we girls need our beauty sleep!*

## Meredith

The other day I was talking to Meredith, a fifteen-year-old girl from Ohio, and I asked her some questions about her life at home. She told me that she has a great family, but then we started talking about some of her friends.

"I can tell when my friends have a broken family."

"How?" I asked.

"Well, my friends who don't live with both parents tend to bail out on me. I'll think we're really close and stuff, but for whatever reason, they'll just leave. It's happened to me a lot."

Certainly this is not true of everyone whose parents are divorced. But it is totally understandable that if a girl has grown up seeing her dad leave her mom, it would be hard to get too close to friends for fear that they will leave just like he did.

Maybe Meredith's friends sound like you. Or maybe your life is more like Tara's. She grew up with a dad who runs the house with force. He's kind of intimidating. To withstand his anger, she learned to be tough. So in relationships, it's tough for her to do that whole emotional thing. Her heart is defensive and calloused.

## How You Look at Adults and Family Members

### Authority

The way you treat adults and family says a lot about your style. I know it sounds boring, but let me tell ya, the more respect we show to the people in charge, the more respect we'll get in return. I know that word *authority* seems intimidating, but I learned something from my good friend Hannah the other day.

Hannah told me that her dad has had the same job for more than twenty-three years. Throughout that time, she can rarely remember him talking negatively about his bosses. Anytime a big project or impossible deadline falls in his lap, he sees it as an opportunity to achieve something he didn't think possible: he views it as a chance to be his best.

Joyce Meyer has a different story. She wrote a book called *Beauty for Ashes* about her life with an abusive father. Because she had a controlling father, she had a warped view of authority. She saw all authority figures as her enemies because her dad had been a scary example of what authority can do.[3] Because of this, she talks about having a difficult time submitting to her husband and how it took years to ever reach the point of respecting her father.

*How do you respond to authority? When teachers assign a major project and set a due date that seems unfair or unrealistic, how do you react? How do you respond to your parents when they ask you to do something you don't feel like doing?*

_____

_____

_____

_____

_____

### How You Look at Your Family

Dads can definitely control the love level in the home.

I remember going on a trip with a friend during spring break in high school. I loved every part of the trip except for those moments when my friend's dad was around. Maybe it was just me, but I felt tension whenever he walked into the room. My nerves were on edge because his temper was on edge. He set the mood in the room. Dads can set a negative tone. Dads can also set a joyful, peaceful tone . . .

## A NOTE FROM MAX

*During the turbulent years of my adolescence, Dad was one part of my life that was predictable. Girlfriends came and girlfriends went, but Dad was there.*

*Football season turned into baseball season and turned into football season again, and Dad was always there. Summer vacation, Homecoming dates, algebra, first car, driveway basketball—they all had one thing in common: his presence.*

*And because he was there, life went smoothly. The car always ran, the bills got paid, and the lawn stayed mowed. Because he was there the laughter was fresh and the future was secure. Because he was there my growing up was what God intended growing up to be; a storybook scamper through the magic and mystery of the world.*

Redefining {beau·ti·ful}

*He made the decisions, broke up the fights, chuckled at the television, read the paper every evening, and fixed break-fast on Sundays. He didn't do anything unusual. He only did what dads are supposed to do—be there.*

*He taught me how to shave and how to pray. He helped me memorize verses for Sunday school and taught me that wrong should be punished and that rightness has its own reward. He modeled the importance of getting up early and of staying out of debt. His life expressed the elusive balance between ambition and self-acceptance.*

*Daddy never said a word to me about sex nor told me his life story. But I knew that if I ever wanted to know, he would tell me. All I had to do was ask. And I knew if I ever needed him, he'd be there.[4]*

## How You Look at Yourself:

Growing up, I watched my friend Liz get comfortable in the shade. But I'm not talking about the quiet shade of an old oak tree. Liz was in the shade of the perfect shadow her older sister had cast with her four-point GPA, her skill in music, her scholarship to a pres-tigious university, her achieved goal of a PhD, and, not to mention, her natural beauty. Liz struggled in school. She jumped from one college to the next, not knowing what she wanted to do, always hanging out in groups of people whose motivation in life was nonexistent. She struggled with insecurities about her weight and frizzy hair. And instead of having a father who encouraged her and her uniqueness, she had a dad who focused on her flaws.

I remember sitting down with Liz one day after another lost battle to drugs. She had already cycled through drug rehab multiple times. During our conversation, I remember her saying that she was finally trying to forgive her dad. I wish we could have talked about it more, but mentally and emotionally, she wasn't ready.

I can't help but wonder if years of not living up to her dad's standards and watching her sister receive all the praise, built insecurity on top of insecurity, contributing to the broken path that she fights to get off of every day.

The way your dad loves or doesn't love you directly impacts how you feel about yourself. Take a minute and think about if your dad's words hurt or help the way you see yourself.

*Because of him, do you feel more beautiful or less beautiful?*

---

---

---

---

---

*Redefining* { beau · ti · ful }

Whether for good or bad, watching how our dads live teaches us how to live, how to have relationships, how to love ourselves. So many of our life accessories—like confidence, contentment and loving others—come from our relationship with dad. But there are no guarantees. Not having a good dad doesn't mean all our relationships are doomed. And having a great dad doesn't mean all our relationships will be perfect.

Our dads *are* going to let us down. So what *was* God thinking? Why did he design us to need a dad's love if that love is not guaranteed to heal all of life's hurts? Big mistake?

Nope.

Perfect plan.

Let's find out why.

*chapter five*

# { the perfect plan }

When your earthly father fails you, your heavenly Father finds you. That's how God's plan stands perfect—no matter what kind of dad you have.

Love from a father doesn't *just* include love from a dad who snores on the couch, pays the cell phone bill, and embarrasses us in front of the boys we have crushes on. Love from a father includes love from one more dad—the perfect Dad.

And he's a Dad who will never make a mistake. A Dad who will never leave us, never forsake us. A Dad who is always kind, patient, and loving—and who never breaks a promise. Nothing, and I mean *nothing*, we could do will ever separate us from his love.

Though our earthly dads will impact who we are, it's only our heavenly Dad's love that can *define* who we are. It's only this Dad's love that can make us complete and fill every need in our hearts. And it's only this Dad's love that can determine whether we see ourselves, others, and God according to the standards of a new kind of beauty—a beauty we may have never known existed. God wants to redefine the concept of beautiful. It's his fingerprints that are the accessories we need; they are the fashion must-haves, and *the* essential elements to our look.

## A NOTE FROM MAX

*God is not blind to your problems. In fact, God is willing to give you what your family didn't.*

**Didn't have a good father? He'll be your Father.**

*Through God you are a son; and, if you are a son, then you are certainly an heir.—Galatians 4:7 (PHILLIPS)*

**Didn't have a good role model? Try God.**

*You are God's children whom he loves, so try to be like him. —Ephesians 5:1 (NCV)*

**Never had a parent who wiped away your tears? Think again. God has noted each one.**

*You have seen me tossing and turning through the night. You have collected all my tears in your bottle! You have recorded every one in your book. —Psalm 56:8 (TLB)'*

God is the best Dad in the world!

He totally completes our look. Getting to know him as our Dad will redefine our look inside and out, making us more and more beautiful.

*Redefining* {beau · ti · ful}

Check out another cool promise:

*How great is the love the Father has lavished on us, that we should be called children of God! And that is what we are!*
— 1 John 3:1

Not having a good relationship with her parents can be a really difficult thing for a girl to overcome, but thankfully, our God is able make any relationship good if we let him. Look at this story about a guy who chose to let God define him, instead of the world and his past.

## A NOTE FROM MAX

*Perhaps your childhood memories bring more hurt than inspiration. The voices of your past cursed you, belittled you, ignored you.*

*And now you find yourself trying to explain your past. I came across a story of a man who must have had such thoughts. His heritage was tragic. His grandfather was a murderer and a mystic who sacrificed his own children in ritual abuse. His dad was a punk who ravaged houses of worship and made a mockery of believers. He was killed at the age of twenty-four . . . by his friends.*

*The men were typical of their era. They lived in a time when prostitutes sold themselves in houses of worship.*

Wizards treated disease with chants. People worshiped stars and followed horoscopes. More thought went into superstition and voodoo than into the education of the children.

It was a dark time in which to be born. What do you do when your grandfather followed black magic, your father was a scoundrel, and your nation is corrupt?

Follow in their footsteps? Some assumed he would. You can almost hear the people moan as he passes, "Gonna be just like his dad."

But they were wrong. He wasn't. He reversed the trend. He defied the odds. He stood like a dam against the trends of his day and rerouted the future of his nation. His achievements were so remarkable, we still tell his story twenty-six hundred years later.

The story of King Josiah. The world has seen wiser kings; the world has seen wealthier kings; the world has seen more powerful kings. But history has never seen a more courageous king than young Josiah.

He flipped through his family scrapbook until he found an ancestor worthy of following. Josiah skipped his dad's life and bypassed his grandpa's. He leapfrogged back in time until he found King David and decided, "I'm going to be like him."

The principle? We can't choose our parents, but we can choose whom we follow.

And since Josiah chose David (who had chosen God), things began to happen.

The people tore down the altars for the Baal gods as Josiah directed.

*Josiah . . . broke up the idols and . . . beat them into powder.*

*He cut down all the incense altars in all of Israel (2 Chronicles 34:4–5, 7, NCV).*

God was his God. David's faith was Josiah's faith. He had found the God of David and made him his own.

An entire generation received grace because of the integrity of one man.

Could it be that God placed him on earth for that reason?

Could it be that God has placed you on earth for the same?

Maybe your past isn't much to brag about. Maybe you've seen raw evil. And now you, like Josiah, have to make a choice. Do you rise above the past and make a difference? Or do you remain controlled by the past and make excuses?

For you to find an ancestor worth imitating, you, like Josiah, have to flip way back in your family album.

If such is the case, let me show you where to turn. Put down the scrapbook and pick up your Bible. Go to John's gospel and read Jesus' words: "Human life comes from human parents, but spiritual life comes from the Spirit" (John 3:6, NCV).

Think about that. Spiritual life comes from the Spirit! Your parents may have given you genes, but God gives you grace. Your parents may be responsible for your body, but God has taken charge of your soul. You may get your looks from your mother, but you get eternity from your Father, your heavenly Father.

By the way, he's not blind to your problems. In fact, God is willing to give you what your family didn't.

Josiah chose to live a life that screamed, "I am a son of God!" Now it's your turn to scream who you are—a beautiful daughter of God (just don't scream so loud it scares the people around you)! That's it! That's all that matters! That's what God sees when he sees you and me! So we shouldn't let anyone define who we are—or whether or not we are beautiful. The only One worthy of telling us who we are is our perfect Dad.

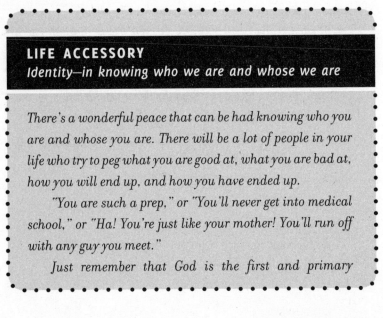

**LIFE ACCESSORY**
*Identity—in knowing who we are and whose we are*

*There's a wonderful peace that can be had knowing who you are and whose you are. There will be a lot of people in your life who try to peg what you are good at, what you are bad at, how you will end up, and how you have ended up.*

*"You are such a prep," or "You'll never get into medical school," or "Ha! You're just like your mother! You'll run off with any guy you meet."*

*Just remember that God is the first and primary*

*authority in your life who can tell you exactly who you are and where you are going.*

*Who does he say you are? His!*

*Where does he say you are going? Wherever he sends you. And girl, he's got BIG plans for you (check out Jeremiah 29:11)!*

God knows exactly what each one of us needs to be the person he created us to be, and he wants to provide every essential for that look. Only he can give us what it takes to be truly beautiful. Check these verses out and see that God not only made you, but he took his time designing your unique and beautiful look.

> *Yet, O LORD, you are our Father.*
> > *We are the clay, you are the potter;*
> > *we are all the work of your hand. —Isaiah 64:8*

> *For you created my inmost being;*
> > *you knit me together in my mother's womb.*
> *—Psalm 139:13*

No dad is perfect, but God sets the perfect example for how we should look at our relationships and ourselves. So we are going to bring your perfect Dad into the relationship picture. Because in order for God to make our relationships with boys, friends, and ourselves more beautiful, we have to make sure to chat about the relationship that matters the most: you and God.

chapter six

{ nice to meet you }

*I* have four soul-mate friends, and they are each so beautiful in their own way. Let me tell ya, I never would have thought that these four girls would be my closest friends. When I met Callie, her hot-pink Capri pants and her coordinating hot-pink and orange–striped top were so bright, I thought I might go blind. Tia and Whitney were practically attached at the hip. They used to keep the entire dormitory hall up until 3:00 a.m. doing late-night calisthenics and playing video games. To this day, they have permanent calluses on their thumbs from playing too much *Super Mario Brothers*. And Beth was so sweet and innocent that I thought I would scare her away with my loud mouth. Her room was always clean, and it always smelled like fresh laundry. Since my idea of doing laundry was spraying Febreze, my room was about as fresh and clean as the fungus under my grandpa's toenails. I never imagined our hearts would connect the way they have.

What I first did with these four amazing girls is what we all sometimes do when we meet people: before I got to know them, I pegged them with a certain label. I am guilty of that all the time!

*She looks like a snob. He looks like a total dork. She looks like a freak.* I automatically assume I know what kind of person he or she must be, just based on appearances.

As I got to know my friends for who they really are, I discovered that Callie inspires me by chasing after her dreams, Tia amazes me with her transparency and her ability to instantly connect with people, Whitney teaches me with advice and godly wisdom, and Beth understands me and always empathizes with my latest struggle.

Our initial impression of a person can sometimes make or break a relationship. Based on my first impression of these four girls, I would have never expected us to become sisters for life. If I hadn't gotten over who *I* thought they were, if I hadn't let *them* show me who they really are, I would have missed out on some of the best relationships I have in my life.

*Think about the first time you met your best friend. What was your initial impression of her? How is that different now that you really know her?*

_____

_____

_____

_____

_____

## God Impressions

*In the same way we judge people by our early impressions, we often do the same with God. What was your initial impression of God? When someone says, "God," what characteristics come to mind right away? Write down a few words that describe God:*

Some people might write *scary*, because they picture a God who throws balls of fire and punishes anyone who doesn't floss before going to bed or—worse—has doubts, sins, and struggles. Others may picture an old guy with a beard. He smiles a lot while he sits on a couch of clouds, but that's about it. He's not very active, and he doesn't really care about being involved in a human being's life. At times I believe in a "Genie in the Bottle" God who should give me anything I want. How we picture God may be based on what other people have said or on what we have imagined him to be like. The real issue is, have you ever truly met him?

## A NOTE FROM MAX

*When my daughter Jenna was six years old, I came upon her standing in front of a full-length mirror. She was looking down her throat. I asked her what she was doing and she answered, "I'm looking to see if God is in my heart."*

*I chuckled and turned and then overheard her ask him, "Are you in there?" When no answer came, she grew impatient and spoke on his behalf. With a voice deepened as much as a six-year-old can, she said, "Yes."*

*She's asking the right question. "Are you in there?" Could it be what they say is true? It wasn't enough for you to appear in a bush or dwell in the temple? It wasn't enough for you to become human flesh and walk on the earth? It wasn't enough to leave your word and the promise of your return? You had to go further? You had to take up residence in us?*

*"Do you not know," Paul penned, "that your body is the temple of the Holy Spirit?" (1 Corinthians 6:19, NKJV).*

*Redefining* { beau·ti·ful }

> *Perhaps you didn't. Perhaps you didn't know God would go that far to make sure you got home. If not, thanks for letting me remind you.'*

If you have never really met the one true God, I would love for you to meet him for the very first time. Some of you may have known God for a while. If so, that's great! Others may not have known you could actually meet God at all. That's okay too! Wherever you are, whoever you are, do me a favor: open your heart to hearing God tell you who he *really* is.

## THE CEILING FAN INTRUDER

I always have to pee in the middle of the night. It makes me so mad! I get so frustrated when my bladder is writhing in pain and wakes me up in the middle of a deep sleep. Part of the reason I hate this is because I'm kind of a sissy at night. I still get a little nervous about shadows on the wall and creaking noises. Sometimes I have to flip on the lamp just to prove to myself there is no scary monster in my room.

One day I was about to walk into my house when no one was home. But before I turned the door handle, I saw a shadow moving inside. I thought an intruder was in the house. I ran to the neighbor's house to ask her to come with me inside. But as soon as we walked toward my door, I realized the ceiling fan was casting a shadow on the wall. So there I was with a neighbor I had never met before, asking her to help me fight off a ceiling fan. Yeah. Kind of embarrassing.

*What is the most embarrassing thing that scared you but that, in the end, wasn't actually scary at all?*

_____

_____

_____

_____

_____

_____

It's so easy to live our entire lives thinking we see God for who he really is. We think we have him all figured out. We think we know God's look—the type of God he is—when, in reality, we haven't allowed him to flip on the light switch. We base our knowledge of him on a distorted shadow rather than on who he says he is.

Sometimes I am too scared to open up my heart to him. I'm too afraid to see God for who he really is because then my life, my beliefs, and everything I think I know could change. I would rather hide behind a God I created in my head, so I can live my life however I want. Too often I settle for my mistaken impression of what

I think God looks like, rather than let him show me the surprising truth about himself.

The cool part is, when we do start to see God for who he really is, amazing things can happen . . .

# iPhone

My mom just purchased an iPhone. You might think, *Wow, it's pretty cool that your mom is so technologically trendy.* Think again.

The iPhone can do almost everything these days. It stores music, movies, pictures, and games. It has apps for playing games, checking your fitness level, finding the nearest Wendy's, working out, making the bed, and filing your nails—all of this and a phone too! (Okay, so I stretched the last two or maybe three iPhone capabilities, but one day it will happen.) With all of these applications at her fingertips, the only thing Mom uses her iPhone for is calling and texting—and the texting was a big step for her. Okay, she is also getting good at checking her e-mail. I've got to give her that.

Anytime I show her a new trick that her phone can do, she gasps, "I didn't know my phone could do that!"

When we let God show us all that he can do—when we stop assuming we know everything about him and let him teach us who he really is—we gasp, "I didn't know my God could do that!"

It's time to turn on the lights, baby! It's time to look beyond the faint shadow of the God you know. It's time to let God teach you and me how he wants us to look at him.

So how does God want us to look at him?

First, God wants us to see him as our Dad.

*Redefining* { beau·ti·ful }

## A NOTE FROM MAX

*It was her singing that did it. At first I didn't notice. Had no reason to. The circumstances were commonplace. A daddy picking up his six-year-old from a Brownie troop meeting. Sara loves Brownies; she loves the awards she earns and the uniform she wears. She'd climbed in the car and shown me her new badge and freshly baked cookie. I'd turned onto the road, turned on her favorite music, and turned my attention to more sophisticated matters of schedules and obligations.*

*But only steps into the maze of thought I stepped back out. Sara was singing. Singing about God. Singing to God. Head back, chin up, and lungs full, she filled the car with music. Heaven's harps paused to listen.*

*Is that my daughter? She sounds older. She looks older, taller, even prettier. Did I sleep through something? What happened to the chubby cheeks? What happened to the little face and pudgy fingers? She is becoming a young lady. Blonde hair down to her shoulders. Feet dangling over the seat. Somewhere in the night a page had turned and, well, look at her!*

*The song stopped and Sara stopped, and I ejected the tape and put my hand on her shoulder and said, "Sara, you're something special." She turned and smiled tolerantly. "Someday some hairy-legged boy is going to steal your heart and sweep you into the next century. But right now, you belong to me."*

*She tilted her head, looked away for a minute, then looked back and asked, "Daddy, why are you acting so weird?"*

*I suppose such words would sound strange to a six-year-old. The love of a parent falls awkwardly on the ears of a child. My burst of emotion was beyond her. But that didn't keep me from speaking.*

*There is no way our little minds can comprehend the love of God. But that didn't keep him from coming.*

*And we, too, have tilted our heads. Like Sara, we have wondered what our Father was doing. From the cradle in Bethlehem to the cross in Jerusalem, we've pondered the love of our Father. What can you say to that kind of emotion? Upon learning that God would rather die than live without you, how do you react? How can you begin to explain such passion?*[2]

We cannot comprehend the God of the universe singing over us, delighting in us, and nudging the angels, saying, "That's my girl. Isn't she beautiful?" But that's the kind of Father we have!

There are two stories that I want to share to show you the kind of father God is. You may have heard them before, but I'd like to tell them in my own words. I promise to help you apply the stories to your own life. Once you do, you will never be the same.

*Redefining* { beau·ti·ful }

So there was this boy named Ishmael. Let's call him Ishy for short.

Well, Ishy had issues—and who wouldn't, being born into the kind of emotional mess he was! His dad, Abram, or, later, Abraham (let's call him Abe) was married to Sarai when he had a baby with Ishy's mom, Hagar. You can only imagine the tension that Ishy's birth caused between Hagar and Sarai. And to make matters worse, they all lived together—one big, dysfunctional family.

*For some of us, it may be easy to resent God because we were born into something of a mess. Maybe you've never met your father. You may, understandably, find it hard to watch your dad have another woman as his wife, a woman who's not Mom. Ishy knew what that feels like. In fact, his situation got worse.*

When Ishy was fourteen, Abe's wife, Sarai, who would later be called Sarah, ended up having a baby boy. For fourteen years, Ishy got all the attention he needed from his dad, and now there was this new kid—this celebrated miracle baby that Abe's wife had never thought she could have.

*What stepsisters, stepbrothers, or half siblings have interrupted your life? Maybe some days you feel like the forgotten child, in second place and needing to compete for Dad's attention. Or your mom and dad might be together, but you still have to fight for his attention.*

Just when Ishy thought life couldn't get worse, Sarai decided that Ishy and his mom needed to leave. After all, Sarai and Abe finally had the son they had always wanted. So she kicked Hagar and Ishy out! Ishy longed to see his dad fight for him. As he walked away with his bags packed, Ishy ached for his dad to run after him, pull him close, and say, "Don't leave! I won't let you leave! Live with me!" But that didn't happen. His dad just stood there and watched them walk away. Ishy kept glancing over his shoulder to get one last look at the dad he would probably never see again. He tried to be tough, but as soon as his dad's face was too distant to distinguish, tears poured down his cheeks.

*Many kids today have a suitcase for Mom's house and a suitcase for Dad's. Every other week they live with a different parent. They hate leaving one, but they love seeing the other. In some of these situations, Dad has a different wife and a new baby. It feels like he chose a different family. Sound familiar? Maybe you've tried to stay tough and tried to convince yourself this doesn't hurt, but it really tears at your heart. You're not alone.*

Hagar and Ishy wandered the desert until their food and water ran out. They had nowhere to go and no one to take them in. We can only imagine that Ishy was mad at his dad, but loved him. Hated his dad, but missed him. Wanted his dad to protect him, to hold him, and to tell him that everything was going to be all right.

*We all long to feel we have someone who will hold us, give us hope, and protect us, but many of us feel we don't have anyone. At those times we may begin to give up on life and even to give up on ourselves. We may also feel lost, struggling with who we are and where we are going.*

When Ishy and his mom were just about to give up, God stepped in. God heard Ishy crying, and the angel of God asked Hagar, "What is the matter, Hagar? Do not be afraid; God has heard the boy crying as he lies there. Lift the boy up and take him by the hand, for I will make him into a great nation"

*Redefining* {beau·ti·ful}

(Genesis 21:17–18). God then gave them water to drink and took care of them.

And that's not all. The Bible says that God was with Ishy as he grew up. God didn't let Ishy grow up without a father. He was Ishy's perfect Dad. He provided for Ishy, protected him, and gave him a dream and a purpose for living. In the end, the Bible says, Ishmael began his own family, and his descendants were numerous.

*This story sheds light on how God is like a father. What dad qualities did God have in the story?*

Circle the phrases that describe the kind of perfect Dad you and I have in God:

*I have loved you with an everlasting love; therefore with loving-kindness have I drawn you and continued My faithfulness to you.* — Jeremiah 31:3 (AMPLIFIED VERSION)

*For in the day of trouble He will hide me in His shelter; in the secret place of His tent will He hide me; He will set me high upon a rock.* — Psalm 27:5 (AMPLIFIED VERSION)

*My father and mother walked out and left me, but God took me in.* — Psalm 27:10 (MSG)

*He fulfills the desires of those who fear him; he hears their cry and saves them.* — Psalm 145:19

## A NOTE FROM MAX

*It would be enough if God just cleansed your name, but he does more. He gives you his name. It would be enough if God just set you free, but he does more. He takes you home. He takes you home to the Great House of God.*

*Adoptive parents understand this more than anyone. We biological parents know well the earnest longing to have a*

Redefining { beau · ti · ful }

> *child. But in many cases our cribs were filled easily. We decided to have a child and a child came. In fact, sometimes the child came with no decision. I've heard of unplanned pregnancies, but I've never heard of an unplanned adoption.*
>
> *That's why adoptive parents understand God's passion to adopt us. They know what it means to feel an empty space inside. They know what it means to hunt, to set out on a mission, and take responsibility for a child with a spotted past and a dubious future. If anybody understands God's ardor for his children, it's someone who has rescued an orphan from despair, for that is what God has done for us.*
>
> *God has adopted you. God sought you, found you, signed the papers, and took you home.*[3]

Throughout the Bible, God asks us to know him as our Dad. Getting to know God as my Dad changed everything for me. It has made my life so much more beautiful. And it can do the same thing for you.

## STORY #2: THE UNTITLED STORY

(This story is so good that I'd be doing it an injustice if I gave it a title. Check out the books Matthew, Mark, Luke, or John for the whole story about Jesus. It's all amazing stuff!)

The thought pained him. He had known from the beginning of time that this day would be a dark one, but he also knew that light was just around the corner.

Thirty-three years had passed on earth since God had sent his Son Jesus to dwell among his creation, and now the day that all of heaven dreaded—and the day hell would rejoice—was here: Jesus would die. Though he had all the power in the world to save his Son, God held back his hand.

*Though you probably don't know what it's like to be a parent, you may have lost a loved one. If not, try picturing what it would be like to lose someone in your family. What if you knew ahead of time that a person you loved was going to die? Wouldn't you want to save and protect that person?*

For Jesus, the distance between heaven and earth was much farther than any move a twenty-first-century family could ever make. And when I say "distant," I don't mean in the sense of miles; I mean distant in terms of . . . well . . . everything. I know we think it's difficult to try to speak a new language or eat unusual food. But Jesus went from royalty to commoner, from having hands that held the stars to hands that hammered wood, from possessing a voice that spoke creation into being to a voice that cracked during puberty. God became man.

It was during these thirty-three years on earth that Jesus announced that he was the Son of God and that, through him, people could have eternal life.

*Imagine being one of the people listening to Jesus' claims. Would you have believed him or thought he was crazy? If I were there and someone asked me what my initial impression of Jesus was, I probably would have said he was a psycho. But at the same time, he definitely had a look about him that would have made me curious. Have you ever met someone kind, with gentle eyes and an inexplicable glow that*

*Redefining* { beau · ti · ful }

*draws you? I would like to think that if I met Jesus on earth, he would be similar to one of those people.*

Jesus performed miracle after miracle. He fed the poor and hung out with the losers no one else liked. But the miracles and kindness were not his sole purpose for leaving heaven and moving into our neighborhood. He had one main purpose—to die.

*I know it stinks to go to detention on a Saturday morning, knowing that three hours of cleaning up the campus await. I know it's a pain to go home after school with a bad report card knowing that Mom is going to ask about it. And I know it's an eye-roller to spend half of the summer at Grandma's house watching reruns of* Jeopardy *all day. But to go somewhere knowing you are going to die there? Now that's a whole other ballgame.*

The amazing part about Jesus' life on earth was that he *chose* to come. He didn't have to!

*I'm pretty sure that if I were living it up in heaven at the right side of God, there's no way I'd volunteer to live thirty-three years on earth, where I'd experience sickness, cruelty, hunger, misunderstanding, rejection, betrayal, loneliness . . . but Jesus came not only to go through all of that, but also—and he knew this—to die and experience utter separation from his Father.*

Jesus didn't have to die on a cross. He could have died a quick, painless death, something less grueling than six hours hanging on a splintery tree. But he died one of the cruelest of deaths so that even the cruelest of our sins could be forgiven.

*Think about the different ways we can sacrifice something for someone. We can give up our weekend and volunteer at a food bank.*

*We can miss our favorite TV show in order to help our sister with her homework. We can give our allowance to a homeless man on the streets. Not necessarily easy stuff, I know. But nothing that we do— nothing that anyone has ever done—can compare to the sacrifice God made.*

Why did Jesus have to die? Well, here's the dilemma: God is perfect. We are . . . well . . . obviously not. Because God is good and just, the right thing to do with all of our mess-ups would be to punish us forever and not let us live with him in heaven. But since God loves us too much to see us die as a result of our sin, he had his Son take our place as a perfect sacrifice, so that all of our sins could be forgiven.

The Bible says that Jesus, who knew no sin (meaning he was perfect), became sin (he took on all of our mistakes) so that through Jesus, God sees us as clean and good (2 Corinthians 5:21).

And just when the demons of hell thought they were victorious because the Son of God was dead, just when the angels were hanging their heads in anguish, the earth began to shake. The guards protecting the tomb of Jesus began to tremble in fear. The stone that blocked the entrance to the tomb slowly began to roll away.

Jesus had risen from the dead! Jesus conquered death and conquered sin for us. Because of Jesus, God has given us the gift of joining his family and living with him forever.

I love a happy ending—I love watching Disney movies for that very reason. But I have never watched or read a story that has as good an ending as this one. In this story, you and I receive the

*Redefining* { beau · ti · ful }

best ending ever: we are adopted daughters of God! Think about that for a minute. You and I are daughters of the same God who created the stars, the same God who invented the concept of breathing, the same God who formed the fish in the sea and the birds in the air! That's our Dad!

*chapter seven*

{ my facebook
addiction }

*I* have an addiction. It's not cigarettes. It's not alcohol. And, no, believe it or not, it's not shopping. I am addicted to Facebook.

If you've never heard of Facebook, let me tell you about it. It's an online networking system where people can keep in touch with friends. People post a profile, put pictures up of themselves, have a message board, and share personal bios.

I can stay up for hours getting lost in my friends' lives on Facebook. I lose myself in my friend's vacation pictures from Hawaii. I feel like I am with her, on the beach, sipping on some coconut milk and giggling when the tide rises high enough to surprise my toes with a cool, salty "hello." I get lost in the pictures from another friend's birthday party that I missed. I hear the guests sing "Happy Birthday" and smell the smoke after she blows out the candle flames dancing on top of her cake.

See? I have a problem! Even now, when I'm not on Facebook, I find myself caught in Facebook's social web just by thinking about it.

Well, all of my time on Facebook got me thinking about

relationships and all the personal options on Facebook's profile. Options like making a "Relationship Status" selection, which gives choices to define one's love life, like: "Single," "In a Relationship," "It's Complicated," and "In an Open Relationship."

Now that we're starting to look at God as our Dad, let's see how a Father/daughter relationship status changes us.

Once we adjust the way we see God and look at him as our Dad, we get a free life makeover. Our look begins to change. We begin to really see ourselves as his daughters. When we have a Dad who calls us beautiful, we begin to see ourselves as beautiful too. But not in the way the world defines *beautiful*. What God helps us recognize is an inner beauty accessorized with security, value, love, self-control, peace, joy, and contentment.

We finally see what God sees when he sees us!

And it doesn't stop there. We also start seeing others the way God sees them. If a friend has turned her back on us, bitterness toward that friend turns into forgiveness. If we always crave attention from guys, those unhealthy longings slowly evaporate because of the attention God gives. That's how God starts to redefine for us what relationships are about.

But here's the deal: we can't assume everything will just *instantly* fall into place. God wants us to spend time getting to *know* him as our Dad. He wants a Father/daughter relationship with us. The more we get to know him as our Dad, the more our life changes.

I'm the first to admit that a relationship with God can seem complicated, so let's talk about this. I promise to make it fun.

Remember all those relationship status options to choose from on the Facebook profile? Well, which of these Facebook relationship statuses would describe your relationship with God today?

*Redefining* { beau·ti·ful }

**Single:** *Thanks, but no thanks. I'm an independent kind of girl, and I don't really care about having a relationship with God.*

**In a Relationship:** *I love God. I try to spend time with him and talk to him about my life. I am trying to get to know him and to let him get to know me.*

**In an Open Relationship:** *I think I believe in God, and I try to love him at times, but I don't want to commit every single aspect of my life to him. I like to do things that God may not be a big fan of—partying on the weekends, messing around with my boyfriend, or dressing in clothes that wouldn't be God's pick. So at home or at church I hang out with God, but at school and on the weekends, I sort of leave him out.*

**It's Complicated:** *I've tried the whole "relationship with God" thing, but it's hard! I can't see him, touch him, or hear him. Sometimes I wonder if he even cares about my life. And the Bible seems so boring!*

Just to show you that a relationship with God can change a life, let me tell you my story.

## CHANGING MY
## RELATIONSHIP STATUS

I grew up a preacher's kid; I heard about God my entire life. My dad would lead what our family called "family devotional time" every night, and he would make the Bible come to life. One time, when he was telling us the story in the Bible about God sending manna from heaven to the Israelites (Exodus 16), Dad actually put Nilla Wafers on the ceiling fans when we weren't looking. When he flipped the fans on, the wafers flew through the air. It was supposed to be manna from heaven, but we knew as soon as the small cookies crashed into our foreheads that Dad had gone no farther than our own pantry to find the "heavenly" snack. All that's to say, I was familiar with the Bible. My parents taught me about God. And I loved it all! I really did! Until . . . high school.

High school was tough. I started not only questioning things, but also rebelling. I turned into the stereotypical rebellious preacher's daughter who snuck out of the house and went to parties to drink and smoke with all my friends. I think because I was tired of my peers making fun of me for my faith, I reached a decision: *I want to be cool. Jesus isn't cool. So I'll ditch Jesus.* In the Facebook world, that would be called changing your status from "in a relationship" to "single."

I felt pretty good about that decision for a while, but after a time, I felt even more lost than before. I didn't know who I was. This new look I was trying on—the cool, life-of-the-party look—wasn't really working out for me. My life was full of drama, confusion, and insecurity. Although on the outside I looked as if I had it all together, the more and more I tried to be popular, the more insecure I felt because I wasn't being my true self. I was being whoever everyone else wanted me to be.

I got so annoyed with my mom every time I left for school.

*Redefining* { beau • ti • ful }

She would stand in front of the door as I was madly dashing for the car and say, "Hang on. I want to read this Scripture over you!" At that point in my life, the Bible was the last book I wanted to read. It had been a long time since my Nilla Wafer days when the Bible brought excitement. Now Bible verses were just a waste of thirty long seconds during my fifteen-minute countdown to get to first period. But I think those times that Mom read God's Word over me ended up helping me a lot more than I realized, because during my junior year, something clicked.

It wasn't a message from God written to me in the clouds. It wasn't a fireworks show in my heart. And it wasn't one big miracle or disaster that changed my heart. It was the steady, constant flow of my parents' prayers, the care of my youth minister, and conversations with Christian friends. Through all of this, God showed me that he was pursuing me and that he wanted to show me something. At the time, I wasn't sure what that "something" was. But I felt like God was telling me, "Hey, there's a lot more to me than you think."

And that was good news, because the parties hadn't worked out for me. They had only led to embarrassing memories of my throwing up in the bathroom. Just so you know, being drunk and covered in vomit is not beautiful. Overall, my attempts to be more popular hadn't helped my life much either. I figured out that I was trying to fit in with people who didn't love me for who I really was, and what's fun about that? The parties I attended, the boyfriends I chose, the friends I hung out with, the small lies I told, the gossip I heard—all of this was slowly changing me into someone I wasn't created to be. And I was ready to figure out who

Jenna Lucado really was! I was ready to live a life of meaning. So the whole *relationship-with-God* thing looked kind of interesting for the first time. I changed my relationship status again, from "single" to "in an open relationship." I allowed God into my life at home and at church, but I still wasn't ready to say bye to a circle of girlfriends who discouraged my faith or to dating guys who didn't love God.

Slowly but surely I started getting sick of who I was, sick of what I was doing, and sick of the people I was hanging out with. I guess I just wanted something more. On one hand, I was trying to learn more about God, but on the other hand, I wasn't living a life that God would approve of. This "open relationship" thing was just confusing my identity and spreading my heart thin. My whole look needed a change. My identity needed a major makeover.

I didn't really know where to start when it came to God. I thought I knew him, but something told me that I didn't actually know him at all. That's when I decided to read the Bible, even though all that black fine print looked scarier than any Dickens novel. But instead of speed-reading through it as I would my English homework, I took it at a slower pace so I could really understand what God was trying to tell me about himself. In fact, in the Bible, King David tells us to "meditate" on God's Word. Does that mean David is asking you to pull out your yoga mat, sit Indian-style, and start humming, "Ooommmm"? No. But King David understood the importance of taking God's words in one at a time, thinking about them, applying them to your life, and soaking in the words day and night. God soon became very real and personal to me.

*Redefining* {beau·ti·ful}

*Meditating daily on God's Word refocuses our minds on what matters. It's a time where we can leave our troubles with him and let him talk for once. Here are few tips:*

- *Get comfortable, but not so comfortable you'll fall asleep. Find a quiet location and wear comfy clothes. You might want to curl up in an armchair or go stretch out on the lawn.*

- *Take a few deep breaths, clear your head (the hardest part), and then read a passage of Scripture. Ask God to help you listen, and then sit quietly when you're finished reading.*

- *Pick a time of day when you can sit as long as you need to. That way, you can really rest in him and let him hold you a minute. Let's admit it: We all need to be little girls in a big daddy's arms. And this is your time to be little again and know he's got you.*

  *This practice will get easier the more you do it. It will ease the strain from your life, which will inevitably ease the strain from your face!*

One of the first chapters in the Bible that changed the way I saw God was Psalm 139. Take the time to read it (even if you've read it a thousand times, read it again), and this time try meditation.

Get somewhere quiet, somewhere you won't be distracted, and listen to what God is saying to you.

## Psalm 139
*A David Psalm*

*GOD, investigate my life; get all the facts firsthand.*
*I'm an open book to you;*
    *even from a distance, you know what I'm thinking.*
*You know when I leave and when I get back;*
    *I'm never out of your sight.*
*You know everything I'm going to say*
    *before I start the first sentence.*
*I look behind me and you're there,*
    *then up ahead and you're there, too—*
    *your reassuring presence, coming and going.*
*This is too much, too wonderful—*
    *I can't take it all in!*

*Is there anyplace I can go to avoid your Spirit?*
    *to be out of your sight?*
*If I climb to the sky, you're there!*
    *If I go underground, you're there!*
*If I flew on morning's wings*
    *to the far western horizon,*
*You'd find me in a minute—*
    *you're already there waiting!*
*Then I said to myself, "Oh, he even sees me in the dark!*
    *At night I'm immersed in the light!"*

*Redefining* {beau·ti·ful}

It's a fact: darkness isn't dark to you;
  night and day, darkness and light, they're all the same to you.
Oh yes, you shaped me first inside, then out;
  you formed me in my mother's womb.
I thank you, High God—you're breathtaking!
  Body and soul, I am marvelously made!
  I worship in adoration—what a creation!
You know me inside and out,
  you know every bone in my body;
You know exactly how I was made, bit by bit,
  how I was sculpted from nothing into something.
Like an open book, you watched me grow from conception to birth;
  all the stages of my life were spread out before you,
The days of my life all prepared
  before I'd even lived one day.

Your thoughts—how rare, how beautiful!
  God, I'll never comprehend them!
I couldn't even begin to count them—
  any more than I could count the sand of the sea.
Oh, let me rise in the morning and live always with you!
  And please, God, do away with wickedness for good!
And you murderers—out of here!—
  all the men and women who belittle you, God,
  infatuated with cheap god-imitations.
See how I hate those who hate you, God,
  see how I loathe all this godless arrogance;
I hate it with pure, unadulterated hatred.
  Your enemies are my enemies!

{ my facebook addiction }

*Investigate my life, O God,*

   *find out everything about me;*

*Cross-examine and test me,*

   *get a clear picture of what I'm about;*

*See for yourself whether I've done anything wrong—*

   *then guide me on the road to eternal life. —Psalm 139 (MSG)*

Psalm 139 helped me realize that this big, "boring," and "ancient" book was actually interesting. And I was amazed how relevant it was to my life! When I felt lonely on the weekends after I decided to stop hanging out with the "friends" that were bringing me down, God reminded me, "Jenna, where can you go where I am not?" And anytime I felt ugly in front of the mirror—and, girl, I know you understand me when I say girls have "ugly days"—I would look at verses 13 and 14 to remind myself that God intricately designed me and that I am a marvelous creation!

Slowly, the Bible came to life for me. I started finding verses that redefined how I saw myself. Instead of thinking I couldn't handle the problems life threw at me, verses like the one in 1 John 4 that says, "You, dear children, are from God and have overcome them [problems], because the one who is in you is greater than the one [the devil] who is in the world" made me feel empowered! (verse 4, NIV).

One night I stayed up late talking to my boyfriend. The lights were out, and he started kissing me. I remember wanting to go along with it, but then I heard words from Romans 12:1 in my head: "Offer your bodies as living sacrifices, holy and pleasing to God." Though it seemed embarrassing at the time (and, trust me, it wasn't easy), I abruptly pushed myself away saying I couldn't

*Redefining* { beau · ti · ful }

make out anymore. I know he thought I was crazy, but that moment redefined my standards when it came to guys.

After that I looked for guys who cared more about encouraging my godly character instead of encouraging me to look or act a certain way because it pleased them. Is that to say I was perfect with my boyfriends after that? No! But it shows that during difficult moments—in a dark room with a boy, in a circle of gossiping girls, in a group that is passing around a joint, even in your own room when you are trying to hurt yourself—God is there, nudging you to make the right choice. He cares about us! All we have to do is listen. And the more I chose to listen to my heavenly Dad, the more my perspective, my standards, and my choices began to change. He made my heart more beautiful than ever before!

I remember the night I lay sobbing into my pillow after hearing heartbreaking news. My Aunt Jana, a young mother of three, had died of a sudden brain aneurysm. As my head swam in a sea of sadness, I begged God for comfort. He gave me psalm after psalm of encouragement. "The Lord is close to the broken" (Psalm 34:18) proved true that very night. At moments like that, I know the Bible works. At moments like that, I realize God really is my Dad, speaking to me and giving me advice. And in those moments, I experience what a relationship with God is all about.

Reading God's Word teaches us more about what kind of Father he is and how we can live as his daughters. It is God's way of talking to us. But, remember, it's just as important for us to talk to him too.

### Texting God

How many text messages do you send your best friend every day? How long do you stay on the phone with a girlfriend or boyfriend? How many notes do you pass in class? We love to stay in touch with our friends, but for some reason, we find it hard to stay in touch with a God who always hears us and who is always there for us!

God longs for us to talk to him about the same things we talk to our friends about. He wants to hear about that friend who turned her back on us, that test we are stressed out about, that boy we have a crush on. He cares about what we care about! Hear what he says: "Give all your worries and cares to God, for he cares about you" (1 Peter 5:7 NLT).

God answers prayers. He wants to be a part of your life. Like a good father, he wants a relationship with his daughter. So will you change your relationship status? Maybe you struggle with living a double life like I did—one foot in the world and one in a relationship with God. Maybe you want nothing to do with him, and I've been there too. Maybe you are bored in your relationship with him. Wherever you fall on the status chart, take a moment to pray about your relationship with him. He wants to be more to you than church, more to you than a beautiful day, more to you than a friend; he wants to be your Dad.

## A NOTE FROM MAX

*When Jenna was two, I lost her in a department store. One minute she was at my side and the next she was gone. I* panicked. *All of a sudden only one thing mattered—I had to find my daughter. Shopping was forgotten. The list of things I came to get was unimportant. I yelled her name. What people thought didn't matter. For a few minutes, every ounce of energy had one goal—to find my lost child. (I did, by the way. She was hiding behind some jackets!)*

*No price is too high for a parent to pay to redeem his child. No energy is too great. No effort too demanding. A parent will go to any length to find his or her own.*

*So will God.*

*Mark it down. God's greatest creation is not the flung stars or the gorged canyons; it's his eternal plan to reach his children. Behind his pursuit of us is the same brilliance behind the rotating seasons and the orbiting planets. Heaven and earth know no greater passion than God's personal passion for you.'*

*Need more confidence? Sick of feeling insecure? Use the space below to write a note to God as if you were text messaging him. Just talk to him like you would your best friend.*

After confessing some insecurities to God, I think it's time to talk about how beautiful he thinks you are!

{ mercedes? $40,000.
mansion? $3 million.
you? priceless! }

*A*wwww man! We have to go to Fredericksburg again?"

My sisters and I dreaded the Saturday mornings my parents announced that we had to load the car for a day in Fredericksburg. This beautiful, quaint, country town, nestled away in the Texas Hill Country, is known for its peaches in the summer and its charming Christmas lights in the winter. Fredericksburg is definitely a storybook sight, but if youd heard our moans and groans, you would have thought Mom was taking us to the dentist's office. What was it that made Fredericksburg miserable for a four-, a seven-, and a nine-year-old girl? Antiques. The equation was simple: Antiques + Mom = A very long, very boring Saturday.

Dad would try to make the trip fun. But we could only play hide-and-seek in a store for so long before getting caught by the store clerks, have so many bubblegum-blowing contests before the gum grew too hard, and play tic-tac-toe so many times before we ran out of strategies. Mom would spend what felt like days in those antique stores!

At the time, I had no idea why anyone would want to buy an old piece of junk. Why was a bed from the 1800s more expensive than a bed made today? Wasn't that concept backward? After all, who wants to sleep in a bed that has been slept in by who knows how many smelly heads before your own?

I couldn't understand the value of antiques.

## Do You Think You Are Valuable?

At one point or another, we have all encountered someone who did not understand our value. Other girls have gossiped about us or laughed at our clothes. Boys have made fun of our hair-cuts or clumsiness in gym class. Even worse, some of us haven't even had family members who have encouraged us, called us beautiful, or said, "I love you." But before we start letting other people determine our worth, it's important to recognize the value that God gives us and how we need to treat ourselves accordingly. Once we understand this, it's a huge step in re-defining beautiful.

When Mom bought an expensive antique, I could not have cared less. I remember being six years old and drawing what were certainly works of art on my bed with a permanent marker, with absolutely no regard for the bed's value. It wasn't a valuable piece of furniture to me; it was a canvas for my marker! I also used to get into my mom's makeup, not caring if I crushed the lipstick or smeared mascara all over the bathroom counter. When we don't understand the value of something, we won't treat it with care. But does that mean that the object is any less valuable? No!

*Redefining* { beau · ti · ful }

Sometimes we can't understand the value of something until someone we trust tells us just how valuable it is.

*What are some treasures you have treated like trash because you didn't yet understand their value?*

---

---

---

{ mercedes? $40,000. mansion? $3 million. you? priceless! }

In the book *Lies Women Believe*, author Nancy DeMoss says we sometimes don't see our value until we hear it from our Creator:

> Someone who does not recognize or appreciate fine art would toss a masterpiece into the trash. Would that make the painting any less valuable? Not at all. The true worth of the art would be seen when an art collector spotted the painting and said, "That is a priceless piece, and I am willing to pay any amount to acquire it."[1]

DeMoss goes on to say, "When God sent His only Son, Jesus, to this earth . . . He declared the value of our soul to be greater than the value of the whole world."[2] Did you read that?! Our value is greater than the value of the whole world! We have a God who calls us valuable! How does that impact the way we look at ourselves? How *should* it affect the way we look at ourselves? Well, once we *believe* in who God says we are, we begin to treat ourselves with value.

We begin to make better choices. We date guys who treat us with respect. We seek help for things like hurting ourselves or hating ourselves. We hang out with friends who encourage us. Pretty soon, we begin to radiate a sparkling beauty because we are confident of our worth. We treat ourselves as masterpieces hand stitched, handcrafted, and hand chosen by the Creator of all that is lovely.

## A NOTE FROM MAX

*Listen closely. Jesus' love does not depend upon what we do for him. Not at all. In the eyes of the King, you have value simply because you are. You don't have to look nice or perform well. Your value is inborn.*

*Period.*

*Think about that for just a minute. You are valuable just because you exist. Not because of what you do or what you have done, but simply because you are. Remember that. The next time someone tries to pass you off as a cheap buy, just think about the way Jesus honors you . . . and smile.[3]*

Seeing ourselves the way God sees us makes it easier to see ourselves as beautiful. Here are three big areas where this impacts your life. I call these the "Three *E*s."

- *External Appearance*

- *Self-Esteem*

- *Expectations*

{ mercedes? $40,000. mansion? $3 million. you? priceless! }

In high school, I had a hard time understanding my worth. I lived to impress my friends and, of course, boys. The worst fights Mom and I had were not about grades, my attitude, or the cleanliness (or lack thereof) of my room. Our World War III was always over swimsuits.

Mom wanted me to cover that, hide this, and conceal those. I wanted to show that, flaunt this, and reveal those. I didn't understand why I was the only one among my friends who couldn't wear a bikini. All my friends told me I should get one, I knew boys liked them, and the magazines told me I had to buy one to be *in*. Every time we went swimsuit shopping, I would leave the mall crying, and my mom would leave rolling her eyes.

"Jenna, you don't understand how boys think," she would say. My comeback would always be, "Well, you're not exactly a boy either, Mom! How do you know what they think?" Maybe you've used that line before. Or how about this one? "Mom, I'm not buying this to show off in front of the guys. It's cute! It's not my fault that they look at me!"

The truth is that my mom was the only one who saw my value in that situation. I couldn't see it, my friends couldn't see it, boys couldn't see it, and of course the magazines couldn't see it. She was the only one who understood that the body God had given me was valuable—something to be treasured, not put on display.

When we look at our body as valuable and handcrafted by God, we will treat it with care. We will treat it the way God wants us to treat it. We will dress it in the way that God asks us to dress it. And how does he want us to dress?

Well, check out this fashion tip in 1 Timothy 2:9–10 (NLT): "And I want women to be modest in their appearance. They should wear decent and appropriate clothing and not draw attention to themselves . . . For women who claim to be devoted to God should make themselves attractive by the good things they do."

Now, don't misinterpret the Bible and think God is saying we have to wear turtlenecks all year round. First of all, that would be ridiculous during the summer heat. Second, and more important, we can still dress cute and stylish in a modest way. God doesn't ask us to drape ourselves in a sheet or not go shopping at Forever 21. He simply asks us to be modest and to help our brothers out by not drawing attention to certain areas of our bodies. If we are showing cleavage or wearing tight clothes that hug our every curve, boys' minds will wander to places they don't need to be, and that will not help them treat us with the respect we want and deserve. When we dress in a way that honors our heavenly Dad, we attract boys of character—boys who care more about our hearts than our bodies.

Think about it this way. If you saw an older woman getting out of a brand-new Mercedes and wearing a tailored black suit, how would you interact with her? You would probably talk in a respectful manner and with a mature tone. You might even bust out a "yes, ma'am." But suppose you're at the beach, and the same woman is in board shorts and a T-shirt, playing Frisbee with her dog. Your interaction wouldn't be quite so formal. Your language would be more relaxed. Her outward appearance would affect how you acted around her.

What we wear says a lot about how we expect to be treated. If a guy notices that a girl is wearing clothes that tease his eyes, he will more than likely think she is a girl who is easy and flirty, and he may treat her with less respect. But if we keep the private places private, guys will think we are a little bit more mysterious. They won't assume that you are someone to take advantage of.

## BEAUTY TIP
### *Modest Is Hottest*

*As a good friend of mine always says, "Modest is hottest." And it's true! Want some tips on how to be trendy and modest?*

- *Keep some cute and colorful cardies to layer over tops that hug your skin a little too tightly.*

- *Buy undershirts and tanks. Nowadays it's all about layering, so put a tank under a low-cut shirt!*

- *With tights in all patterns and colors, keep some in your closet to go under skirts or even shorts that you think (or your mom thinks) are a little too short. Really, with all the options out there, why go for a really short pair of shorts or skirt when you are just going to be self-conscious the whole time anyway?*

*Redefining* { beau · ti · ful }

My younger sister Andrea walks gracefully at five feet ten inches tall. She has the most beautiful, thick, shiny head of strawberry blonde hair—it puts Nicole Kidman to shame. A constellation of cute freckles dusts her cheekbones and the top of her nose. A few months ago she moved to Oxford, England, to get her master's degree in English literature. How cool is she, right? I have always admired her confidence and her willingness to step outside of her comfort zone. But if Andrea were sitting next to you right now, she would quickly say that she has not always felt confident. Growing up, she struggled with self-esteem issues like most of us do.

I remember on one of our morning commutes to middle school in Dad's car, Andrea started crying. Baffled, Dad and I asked her why she was upset. I filed through the potential problems in my head: homework she forgot to do, a test she didn't study for, a friend who was hurting her feelings. Finally, through sobs, she managed to leak out the cause of her misery: "I forgot my face powder!"

At this particular phase in Andrea's life, she really hated her freckles, and she hated that she had rosy cheeks. So every morning she would attempt to cover her "flawed" face with layers of Clinique powder. I tried to get her to stop crying by telling her that crying would make her face redder than it already was, but my eighth-grade, very nonempathetic advice received a rightfully deserved "You don't know what it's like to be red, Jenna!" (Andrea has always been what I call a "drama mama," but shhhh! Don't tell her I told you!)

In addition to hating her face, Andrea struggled for a long

time to accept her height. She was taller than a lot of the boys at our school. She was forever looking for flats for her formals, and every time we shopped for jeans, Andrea went home disgusted that none of the pant legs were long enough.

I remember the light switch flipping on in Andrea's life when she was a sophomore in high school. It wasn't an overnight transformation, but she definitely experienced a gradual change of heart.

She began to care less about her makeup, her height, and even her "friends" who weren't accepting her. Her attitude was more relaxed, and problems she used to see as life threatening became life building. I remember walking into her room one night and finding her reading the Bible by lamplight. I told her that I could see a change in her heart, and she agreed. She told me how spending time with God had really helped her.

Andrea had begun looking at herself the way God looks at her, and everything about her changed. She embraced her height and walked tall; she welcomed the freckles and accepted her rosy cheeks. When we look to God as our Father and really believe that we belong to him, our self-esteem reaches new heights. When we spend time with him, his voice of truth trumps the world's voice of lies as he reassures us, "You are mine! And you are beautiful!"

Take some time right now and tell God about all of your insecurities. He wants to hear about your acne. He wants you to tell him about frizzy hair, feelings of inadequacy, and making the junior varsity team instead of the varsity. Hand over all your insecurities, and take on your true identity as a beautiful daughter of the King of kings. Trust me, it will be a great look for you!

*Redefining* { beau • ti • ful }

*If you live your life comparing yourself to every other girl who walks by, you will never be content with who you are. There will always be girls who are prettier, girls who are smarter, and girls who appear to be more successful. I'm pretty sure I'm not the only girl in the world who has ever picked up a magazine and thought,* Wow! I wish I looked like her. *So anytime you have the urge to compare yourself to someone else, start listing everything about your life that you are thankful for. Ask God to help you do what Paul says in Philippians 4:11: "I have learned to be content whatever the circumstances." God made you to be you for a reason, so learn to love you!*

## YOUR EXPECTATIONS WILL CHANGE

The other day, when I was chatting with a wise mentor of mine, I started asking her about her childhood. Looking at her gentle eyes and knowing her loving soul, I would have never guessed that she had grown up with an alcoholic father. She told me that she and her brothers and sisters feared the nights he would come home drunk. Though he never hurt her, night after night she heard her helpless mother's screams. Whenever her father left town for work, a sigh of relief flooded the home. Her mother would celebrate by baking homemade bread. With a nostalgic smile, my mentor remembered the aroma greeting her at the door after school. "We always knew Dad was gone when we smelled fresh bread." To this day, the smell warms her with peace.

Because of her experience watching her mother take abuse from her dad, she entered her own marriage fully expecting to be abused. Before she said, "I do," she had planned her response to the first time her husband hit her. Her expectations of what a marriage would be were so low because her parents' model of marriage was so dark. My mentor had never had anyone tell her how valuable she was, how much potential she had, or how she deserved to be treated. No one had shown her what true love looks like. No one had ever told her that she deserved the best, so she expected the worst. Tragically, her lack of self-worth led to an abusive marriage that ended in divorce.

She told me that it wasn't until she was around fifty years old that she could understand her worth in God's eyes. Now she lives her life with hopeful expectations, and she doesn't settle for anything less than God's best for her. She even found the love of her life—a man who treats her like a princess.

*It's too easy to settle for less than God's best because of a negative experience or influence in life. Take some time to write down some low expectations you have. They could be anything from not studying because you expect to fail, dating the wrong guy because you don't think the right guy could ever like you, or even not applying to your dream college because you're afraid you won't get accepted.*

*Redefining* { beau · ti · ful }

_____

_____

_____

_____

God doesn't want us to settle for so little. He wants his daughters to soar higher than we could ever dream! He wants to carry us to places we have never been. He wants to dream for us. So will you let him? Don't set your own goals. Let God set them for you! Listen to what he says about the life he promises his daughters if we choose to live by his standards:

> I can do everything through him who gives me strength.
> — Philippians 4:13

> "Be strong; show what you're made of! Do what God tells you. Walk in the paths he shows you . . . then you'll get on well in whatever you do and wherever you go." —1 Kings 2:2–3 (MSG)

> Do what you're told so that you'll have a good life, a life of abundance and bounty, just as GOD promised, in a land abounding in milk and honey. — Deuteronomy 6:3 (MSG)

Once you start seeing yourself as God's daughter, he redefines your expectations, your self-esteem, and even your external appearance.

*chapter nine*

# { "hello! my name is _____" }

*A*ll of us have names and nicknames that people use to catch our attention, but we have other names too—names for ourselves that only we know, names that only we use. If you walked into a party and were asked to fill out a name tag—you know, the standard blue stickers that say, "Hello! My name is _____"—what name would you put in the blank?

I'm not talking about the name your mom and dad gave you, because let's just admit it—we can be our own worst enemies. Sometimes, we give ourselves terrible names! A name that I call myself a lot is "Idiot." Anytime I make a mistake, I find myself thinking, *Idiot! Why did you do that?* I went through a season where my name for myself was "Fat." At times, I have also called myself names that other people called me as well, or names that I *thought* they called me. When I wasn't invited to parties, I became "Outsider." And when I didn't get elected president of the student council, my name changed to "Loser."

Stop and take some time to think about the names you call yourself and the names others have called you that you may have unknowingly used to define yourself. Fill in the blanks below:

*"Hello! My name is* _____*."*

*"Hello! My name is* _____*."*

*"Hello! My name is* _____*."*

*"Hello! My name is* _____*."*

The scary thing is that we have the potential to become the names we call ourselves or that other people call us, especially the ones that the people at home call us. So if we are not called "Beautiful," "Smart," and "Kind," our self-esteem starts to weaken. Even if we have parents who call us endearing names, there are times when we need something more. There are times when peoples' words aren't enough, when they aren't what we need, or when they just don't make us feel better. That's why it's so important to constantly read the names on the tags God has for us. *God has a name tag for me?* You better believe it!

Let's say God decides to host a big party, and you are on the guest list. Wow, just imagine what kind of party God could throw! What's on the menu? Well, what's *not* on the menu? After all, you have your own personal chef at *this* party. Want three courses of macaroni and cheese? Sure! Coming right up! But if those yellow noodles are far too boring, why not try the salade d'endives aux noix et Roquefort for starters, followed by a soufflé au Fromage Raie aux câpres, Pommes vapeur, and end with a nice French brioche. (Wow, I have no idea what I just wrote, but if you are a snobby eater, I may just have spoken your language.)

And because dessert is the best part of a meal, God decides to have a little fun with the final course. He puts Charlie and his chocolate factory to shame. It's a sweet tooth's wonderland. There's a room with a chocolate playground where the dinner guests can go down a chocolate slide, tongue first! Next door are pyramids of cookies and a milk fountain that shoots milk higher than the waters at the Bellagio Hotel in Las Vegas. Love ice cream? Well, put on your parka and step into the Ice Cream Sculpture Room, where you are surrounded by life-size ice cream sculptures. You can take a scoop of rocky road shaped into a giraffe, lick vanilla bean in the shape of a swan, or sit in a sculpted sleigh made of mint chocolate chip.

After the eating, it's time to play! Love to play in the sun? Well, walk on in to the Summer Is Funner Room! There you will find lakes the size of Texas, beaches for those who prefer the sand, theme parks, bikes to ride, boats to sail, canoes to float, and boards to surf. But if summer isn't your favorite season, choose from one of the three other rooms: Fall into Bliss, Winter Wonders, and It's a Spring Thing.

Okay, I am having way too much fun daydreaming about some made-up party. Now, where were we? . . . Oh yeah. The name tag.

So you walk into this party, and everyone has to wear a name tag. Only this time you get to choose from a list of names God calls you. Let's take a look at some of those names that God gives us in the Bible. These names declare who we are in Christ. Go ahead and read about some names you may have never even known you had.

### "Hello! My Name Is Confident."

*Those who fear the LORD are secure.* — *Proverbs 14:26 (NLT)*

*Have no fear of sudden disaster . . . for the LORD will be your confidence.* — *Proverbs 3:25–26*

*For we do not have a high priest [Jesus] who is unable to sympathize with our weaknesses. . . . Let us then approach the throne of grace with confidence, so that we may receive mercy and find grace to help us in our time of need.* — *Hebrews 4:15–16*

### "Hello! My Name Is God's Delight."

*"The LORD your God is with you,*
    *he is mighty to save.*
*He will take great delight in you,*
    *he will quiet you with his love,*
    *and he will rejoice over you with singing."* — *Zephaniah 3:17*

### "Hello! My Name Is Daughter of God."

*For you did not receive a spirit that makes you a slave again to fear, but you received the Spirit of sonship [daughtership]. And by him we cry, "Abba, Father." The Spirit himself testifies with our spirit that we are God's children.* — *Romans 8:15–16*

### "Hello! My Name Is Forgiven."

*"Abraham was declared fit before God by trusting God to set him right." But it's not just Abraham; it's also us! The same thing gets said about us when we embrace and believe the One who brought Jesus to life when the conditions were*

*Redefining* {beau·ti·ful}

*equally hopeless. The sacrificed Jesus made us fit for God, set us right with God. — Romans 4:23-25 (MSG)*

*"But everyone who believes in this raised-up Jesus is declared good and right and whole before God." —Acts 13:38 (MSG)*

## LIFE ACCESSORY
### Value—knowing we are treasured

*Stepped into a Tiffany's jewelry store lately? Tiffany's is in the business of taking your breath away. Counter after counter lined with diamonds and jewels makes every girl gasp, not to mention drool. The way a twenty-karat diamond takes your breath away is the same way you take God's breath away every time he looks at you. The way your eyes twinkle at an unblemished, perfectly clear diamond is the way God's eyes twinkle when he sees you. Because of Jesus, the hard rock of sin that surrounded you was chiseled away, turning you into the most valuable of gems. No matter what mistakes you have made or how many people have told you that you don't amount to anything, know this: you are treasured by the Creator of the stars. He loves you!*

*So if you struggle with knowing you are valuable, march up to the Tiffany's window and say to yourself, "I'm more important to God than the finest of diamonds." And keep saying it until you believe it.*

When we live by the names our heavenly Dad gives us, our look changes. As we learn to see ourselves the way God sees us, we view ourselves with a healthier self-esteem and a greater sense of self-worth. God looks at you, his precious daughter, with genuine pride. In fact, I bet if God drove a car, your picture would be on his dashboard.

## A NOTE FROM MAX

*God loves you just the way you are. If you think his love for you would be stronger if your faith were stronger, you are wrong. If you think his love would be deeper if your thoughts were deeper, wrong again. Don't confuse God's love with the love you get from people. Love from people often increases with performance and decreases with mistakes. Not so with God's love. He loves you right where you are.[1]*

## BEAUTY TIP
### Say Your Names

*A great way to counteract our own negative thoughts toward ourselves is to replace them with positive ones.*

*Redefining* {beau·ti·ful}

*Find a piece of paper or a note card and make a name tag with a verse from this chapter—or several name tags with several verses if you'd like. These name tags can be put on your bedroom or bathroom mirror as reminders of who you really are. Decorate a name tag, attach a string to it, and then hang it on your rearview mirror or stash it in your backpack. Do whatever you need to do to remind yourself of the names God has for you.*

I hope after reading about how much God loves you, your self-esteem tank is overflowing! Okay, so we've chatted about how a relationship with your perfect Dad gives you all the life accessories you need, and now it's time to show those accessories off in our relationships. Let's talk about boys!

# { cindy didn't settle }

*D*id you ever want to be a Disney princess? Growing up, I dreamed about living in Cinderella's Castle at Disney World. That is, until I actually got to go inside the castle and found out it was just a dumb restaurant . . . In the summers I would stick both of my feet through a diving ring at the pool and pretend I had mermaid fins just like Ariel. When Dad got in the pool, he used to dance with us and sing Sleeping Beauty's song "Once Upon a Dream." Anytime he sang the word *you*, he would toss us in the air. I used to walk around with my Fisher-Price karaoke machine singing Ariel's famous underwater solo, "Part of Your World."

Even if you've never dreamed of being a Disney princess, something in all of us wants to be treated like one. Take the "ss" off *princess*, and there's the number one reason behind the princess dream: The Prince. Who doesn't want a good-lookin' prince to ride off into the sunset with! (Personally, I'm afraid of horses, so I'd be okay with driving off into the sunset in a stretch Hummer with a sunroof. But that's just me.)

*What is your perfect prince like? How does he treat you in your dreams? How does he treat others, and what are some of the qualities he would have? Take a minute and write down what kind of man you want to marry someday. Then consider whether your list would match God's list. Have fun with this! Be creative—and be as specific as you want!*

*Redefining* { beau · ti · ful }

I think God loves it when we dream. In fact, I like to think that dreaming is God's reminder to us to not settle for less than his best in our lives. God longs to lavish blessings on us, his daughters.

*In him we have redemption through his blood, the forgiveness*
*of sins, in accordance with the riches of God's grace that*
*he lavished on us with all wisdom and understanding.*
*—Ephesians 1:7–8*

God—our heavenly Dad—doesn't want us to settle for a guy who brings us down, makes us feel uncomfortable, and changes us into a girl he has not created us to be. That's not a prince! A prince loves us for who we are; he challenges us to be a better person; he has integrity; he is a leader; and, if he is a true prince, he knows God as his King.

## CINDY'S STORY

Cinderella—we'll just call her Cindy—didn't settle. The end of the fairy tale says, "They lived happily ever after" because Cindy waited for her prince. Did Cindy ever sneak out of her room in the attic to go meet men at the clubs or bars downtown? Nope. Did she yell at her evil stepmother for not letting her date? Nope. Instead, she humbly accepted her tasks at hand and waited in hope, knowing her dreams would come true. After she met her fairy godmother and rode in her pumpkin limo to the ball, did she catwalk up to the prince and give him her digits (her address digits, of course, since they didn't have cell phones), ask him to dance, and flirt with him to let him know she was available? No way! This prince had to step it up to win Cinderella. *He* noticed her, *he* asked her to dance, and then, after she left, *he* sent a search party to find her. Talk about a man who knew how to pursue his treasure! *Sheesh!*

Let's pause here and say what we are all thinking: "Wow, Cindy had it made!" Doesn't the prince sound a lot like what you long for one day? Handsome, noble, respected, handsome, financially stable (and I do mean *stable*), a good dancer, and—did I mention—handsome? But one of the best qualities the prince had was the confidence necessary to pursue Cindy. Why would any of us want a guy *we* have to chase? Think about it. Don't we want a guy who will work hard to win us over and who will do everything it takes to romance us? After all, if he doesn't have to put any effort into getting us, why would he put any effort into keeping us? Who wants a lazy guy who stops wooing us after he has us? Wouldn't it be wonderful to have a man who, even after thirty years of marriage, is still chasing you?

## My Prince Charming

I met Brett when I was eighteen years old. The first time we shook hands, my stomach did more loopy-loops than a Six Flags roller coaster. I wanted to swim in his sparkling blue eyes. He had tall, broad shoulders and the cutest freckles I'd ever seen! For our first date, he asked me to go to the planetarium. I know you may be thinking, *How dorky is that!* But listen to this. Brett did an entire star-themed date. He bought me *Star*bucks, took me to Lone*star* Café, and even bought me socks with *stars* on them! We started hanging out more, and he even called my dad asking for permission to date me. That blew my mind! I had never had a guy do that. (Talk about scoring points with the parents, right?)

Besides his humor, his passion for God, and his creativity, I loved the questions he asked me. That may sound weird, so let me explain. Before, I felt like I was always the one asking guys about their lives, their day, their family, and pretty much everything. But I had found a boy who asked *me* about me! He was interested in my life. It was so refreshing! But at the time, it was a little too refreshing. I got scared. I was too young to have found this great guy I could see myself with forever. So I chickened out. I wanted to live my life, date other guys in college, and work toward my career. I couldn't get married!

But while I ran away from Brett, he ran toward me. He pursued me. He wrote letters telling me he would wait until I was ready. But it wasn't in a freaky, stalker kind of way. He didn't choose to put his life on hold. He didn't mope around as if his world revolved around me, because it didn't. He simply waited for me for not one, not two, but five long years! I know. Go ahead and slap me. But I know God grew us separately so that we could grow together in his perfect time. Sure enough, on 8/8/08, my prince proposed to me, and you better believe I said yes!

Brett was patient. He pursued me. But most of all he prayed. He trusted God to take charge of our futures.

Wait on God, and pray about the future. God may want to surprise you with the man of your dreams, but he also may want to shower you with blessings in another way. Not all of us are meant to marry, and that's okay. So don't ever force a relationship just to have a boyfriend. Don't settle for a guy who isn't a prince. Instead, wait on God just as Brett waited on God for me. God's number one goal is to draw you closer to him. He knows exactly what your heart needs. So what's your first step? To trust your heavenly Dad.

## Cindy's Dad and Your Dad

I think an important detail about Cinderella's life—a detail we easily forget—appears in the first scene of the story. There we see Cindy as a little girl with a daddy who loves her very much. Unfortunately, he didn't live long, and Cindy was left with an evil stepmother. I would dare to say, though, that the few years of having a father tell her that he loved her and that she was beautiful were enough to plant in her heart the truth, "I am valuable. I deserve the best."

Okay, so I realize I just psychoanalyzed Cinderella, but I think her story aligns with your perfect Dad's dream for you. Read the verse below to see what your heavenly Dad wants for you.

> *"For I know the plans I have for you," declares the* Lord, *"plans to prosper you and not to harm you, plans to give you hope and a future." —Jeremiah 29:11*

We have a God who dreams big for us! So how should this verse affect our guy standards? We should never date a guy who doesn't match God's plan for us—a plan to prosper us, a plan to bring us hope. If we let God set the standard for how we are to be treated, then we'll need to wait for a guy who will try to love and honor us the way our perfect Dad does. Forget the man of your dreams. Wait for the man of God's dreams!

Maybe you haven't been dreaming big because the husband you see your dad being is far from dreamy. Or maybe you have really high standards from watching your dad, and you are waiting on a guy who is as good as he is.

*Redefining* {beau·ti·ful}

*How has your earthly dad affected your dating standards:*

_____

_____

_____

## BEAUTY TIP
### Date Clothes

*The key to a good first date? Comfort. The more you are comfortable with yourself, the less awkward the night will be. One way to help you act comfortably is to dress comfortably. I'm not saying show up in sweats, but this is what I suggest:*

· *Wear something that feels comfortable to sit in.*

· *Wear something that is easy to get in and out of a car in.*

· *Wear something that won't show stains in case of a dinner spill.*

· *Wear something that won't show sweat stains (nerves makes some girls sweat).*

> *The less you have to think about your outfit, the more you can be yourself!*

## SMELLY BOYS COME FROM GOD TOO

Though it's hard to imagine it, in spite of their gray-stained socks, smelly rooms, and hairy toes, boys were created by the same God who created us girls. It's true! They are God's sons. And God is asking us, his daughters, to look at his sons the way he does and to treat them with the same respect and love that we ourselves want.

To honor boys, then, you and I have to understand the role God gave guys so that we can help them be the best men they can be.

Consider the following scenarios and choose the one that would best honor a guy:

1.  You found out that this guy likes you, but he's just too shy to tell you, so you decide to make it easy for him by telling him that you like him before he says anything to you.

2.  You meet this guy that you think is really cool and cute, so you start flirting with him over texting. That way he'll know you are interested.

3.  You have a major crush on this guy, and you've heard that he may like you back, but you decide to let him make the first move. Though waiting is really hard, you think this will be a good time to get to know him as a friend first.

It's important to let the guy pursue you, so that you are sure you're attracting a confident guy, not a lazy one. Like my friend Chad says, "As much as guys want to act confidently, it takes a lot of nerve to ask a girl out. So let us do the work. We're building up a confidence muscle. It's not a good idea to keep guys from building the muscles that we will need all our lives anyway."[1]

We girls need to do our part to help boys learn how to be men, how to be leaders and pursuers. If we make it easy on them by making ourselves too available (physically or emotionally), they won't ever learn how to grow up.

### Don't Trip a Boy

God asks us to not make our brothers stumble. In 1 Corinthians 10:32, he speaks to us through Paul and says, "Do not cause anyone to stumble." Now, does that mean we shouldn't trip a boy down the stairs? Nope—although God probably wouldn't be thrilled about that either. What "Do not cause anyone to stumble" means is that we girls have to be careful *not* to make it easy for guys to lust after us, treat us like dirt, and drift far away from what God has called them to be. Excessive flirting and dressing provocatively—these things make boys' hearts stumble.

So take a second right now and think about your reputation with guys. Are you the girl all the boys like but can't have? Are you the girl who is cruel to boys? Are you the girl who will say "yes" to any guy, so you're asked out all the time? Are you the girl who is kind to everyone but mysterious to boys? Are you the type of girl who gets tired of being *just friends* with guys and is tempted to try harder to get noticed?

Step back and think about how you act around guys, look

around guys, and talk to guys. Now ask yourself if the way you are around guys could make them stumble or make their thoughts wander to places they shouldn't go. Are you helping them build their confidence muscle, or are you making relationships too easy for them? If you look at guys the way God wants you to look at them—as his sons—your relationships with them will be entirely new and much healthier.

We girls need to be aware of what we wear and how we flirt or interact with guys. Hopefully, this new awareness will prompt us to redefine our look, whether it's our fashion choices or our inner style. Choosing to wear modest clothes, talking about stuff that is clean and uplifting, letting the boy initiate—these actions can help boys become true princes and help us be the princess, the priceless treasure worth pursuing. But none of this will happen if the two of you don't know and obey God as your Dad.

## LIFE ACCESSORY
### Self-Control—for making good decisions

*Self-control can be used in every area of our lives. Whether it's restraint from stomping away from our parents or slamming the door on our sister. But let's get really honest. Our relationships with boys ususlly require the most self control.*

*Raging hormones cause a bit of a problem. I know how*

*it feels to have all these crazy hormones and feelings for someone. And we're supposed to just ignore them?!*

*Prayerfully covering ourselves with self-control will not take the hormones away. Sorry, but it won't. But what it will do is help us make good decisions. It will help us avoid situations that could compromise our standards and that make our hormone problem worse. It will help us avoid doing things we will regret, and things our husbands will regret! Remember that perfect prince you wrote about? He just might be out there waiting for you, and there's nothing more beautiful to Prince Charming than a princess who, at some point in her life, stopped and said, "You know what? I'm going to protect my heart and my body for my God, my future prince, and for myself."*

## Crowns over Clowns

There are a lot of royal jerks out there. So to help a sister out, I want to help you know when a guy is a true prince.

A true prince models his life after the King of all kings, God himself. So anytime you question whether or not a guy is going to have charming character, ask yourself, "Does he treat me like my heavenly Father would treat me?" Forget asking friends, watching Hollywood relationships, or looking it up online. The "Is This Boy a Prince?" test is found in the Bible! One of the best places to find out whether a guy will treat you well is 1 Corinthians 13:4–7:

*Love is patient, love is kind. It does not envy, it does not boast, it is not proud. It is not rude, it is not self-seeking, it is not easily angered, it keeps no record of wrongs. Love does not delight in evil but rejoices with the truth. It always protects, always trusts, always hopes, always perseveres.*

This passage describes how God loves us, but I think it's also a useful tool to use as a standard when we're questioning a potential relationship, when we have a crush on a guy, and when we're dating a guy. Now, are we going to find a guy as perfect as God? No! No such thing! But our perfect Father sets the perfect example of what true love looks like, so it's our job to use him as the gauge for how to love and how to be loved.

## A NOTE FROM MAX

*When Jenna was five, two ten-year-old boys walked up to her on the bus, scowled at her, and demanded that she scoot over.*

*When I came home from work, she told me about it. "I wanted to cry, but I didn't. I just sat there—afraid."*

*My immediate impulse was to find out the names of the boys and punch their dads in the nose. But I didn't. I did what was more important. I pulled my little girl up into my lap and let her get lost inside my arms and told her not to worry about those old bullies because her daddy was here,*

*Redefining* { beau · ti · ful }

> *and I'd make sure if any thugs ever got close to my princess*
> *they'd be taking their lives in their own hands, yessir.*
> *And that was enough for Jenna.*[2]

God definitely cares about how we look at guys *and* about how guys look at us. Let him be the example of how to look at boys and how to be looked at by boys. God's plan for our relationships with boys—which brings less drama and less heartache—is a lot more beautiful than the world's. So ask God for boy advice. After all, that's what a dad is for.

Let's wrap up this chapter with a prayer:

*God, thank you for being my Dad. And since you are my Dad, I ask you to redefine my look. Help me see boys the way you want me to see them. May I see them as your creation. Give me the grace to center my relationships on you. Give me patience to wait on your best for my life.*

# { deepwater friendship }

Rachel was my best friend growing up. We played for hours in our own Rachel-and-Jenna world. Some days we became teachers and transformed my bedroom into a classroom. On other days we slid down the stairs in our sleeping bags. But one of our all-time favorite things to do was play with Barbies.

We were Barbie architects, building entire Barbie towns and mansions using the only building materials we had: books. We would stack the books, open the books, lean the books—whatever it took to create the Barbie house or building we wanted. The Barbie Dream House had nothing on us (though we both secretly wanted one!). It would take us three hours to set the scene for our Barbies. Once we created just the right setting, the Barbie story would begin. The screenplays we created for our Barbies read like soap operas. I remember a time when Rachel's Barbie died of cancer, and we both started crying, literally! I think we were a tad obsessed with Barbies. Okay, maybe more than a tad.

Rachel and I had our ups and downs, but one thing I loved and still love about her is that we can pick up where we left off, no matter how much time has passed since we last talked. And I have always felt the freedom to be totally, utterly myself when I am with her. She knows me inside and out, and she loves me in spite of my flaws. I don't have to impress her. I can even pick my nose in front of her, and she still loves me!

*Do you have a best friend? Why is that person your best friend? What are some of your favorite qualities about that friend? If you don't have a close friend right now, what are some of the characteristics you hope for in a friend?*

*Redefining* { beau · ti · ful }

God wants to be a part of our friendships. He knows first-hand what it's like to want friends. Don't believe me? Think about the apostles. Jesus knew he would need a small community of men to hang out with, to encourage and be encouraged by, to love and be loved by. And he wants the same for us. God wants to see his daughters surrounded by friends who help us become the best *we* can be, and he wants to use us in the lives of our friends. He wants to make your friendships better. But how? Well, by redefining the way we look at friendships.

## Under the Sea

Have you ever gone to the beach and played in the ocean? If you are anything like me, you may be a little scared of the deep, endless underwater world. For some reason whenever I first dip a toe in the ocean, an automatic alarm goes off in my head. It's not a typical beeping alarm. It's a warning siren that blasts the theme music from *Jaws*—da-dum, da-dum . . .

My family, on the other hand, is the complete opposite of me. Anytime we go on vacation to the beach, they all want to snorkel (well, minus my mom, who enjoys watching us from afar as she sips her smoothie and tans her legs). I usually want to stay with Mom, but a couple of times I have stared my fear in the face and said, "You aren't stealing my fun today!" It usually works. Try it sometime.

The first time I snorkeled out in the deep, "big girl" water (that's what I call it because I have to put on my big-girl bravery), I realized how much I had missed by staying in the shallow water. It's an entirely new and beautiful world when you go deeper into the ocean. There are pearly-white reefs and fish dressed in all sorts of bright neon greens, oranges, and yellows. Even the slippery seaweed seems to glow. I remember thinking as I snorkeled—one eye on the lookout for sharks—*Wow, if I had never left the shallow beach, I would have never discovered the wonders of the deep waters!*

The same thing happens when you and I let God take our relationships from shallow to deep, from plain to wondrous, from ordinary to exciting. How? Well, when we let God be our Father, he helps us look at friendships the way he intends them to be—encouraging, loving, and life building.

## A NOTE FROM MAX

*A friendship-preserving devotion cannot be found in our hearts. We need help from an outside source.*[1]

### LOOKING AT FRIENDS WITH GOD'S EYES

In the Bible our perfect Dad gives us advice about friendship through a beautiful story about two guys named Jonathan and David. If you're interested in reading the entire story, check out 1 Samuel 18–20.

Most people have probably heard of David, the famous Old

Testament king of Israel. Jonathan, his best friend, usually doesn't get all that much attention. But the truth is, if it weren't for Jonathan, David would never have lived long enough to be a king. You see, David had more drama in his life than Rachel's and my Barbies ever had! Just consider this scandal:

King Saul, Jonathan's dad, grew jealous of David's popularity and saw David as a threat to his throne. So Saul decided to kill David. Can you imagine? David had done nothing except help the king by winning battles and killing their archnemesis, Goliath, yet Saul decided to kill David because his face was on the cover of *Israel Today* (a really popular magazine back then that I may or may not have just made up) and Saul's wasn't.

This isn't all that different from the popularity fight going on right now at any school in the nation. People will do something malicious or watch someone else do something selfish in order to gain popularity. Gossip and betrayal sneak around the lockers and pop up in classrooms, but I hope you have never seen someone try to kill another person for the sake of popularity. Unfortunately, that is exactly what is going on in our story. This is the movie *Mean Girls* times a hundred.

The unsung hero of the story is Jonathan—who was nothing like his father, Saul. He saw his dad's evil heart and decided to save David's life. You think James Bond is pretty sly? Think again! Jonathan, a total insider, snuck out to warn David of his father's plot to kill him. Jonathan put his life on the line for his friend.

Do you have a Jonathan in your life? Are you a Jonathan to someone else? Take a minute to think about the sacrifice Jonathan offered out of love for David, and compare it to your own friendships. I hope you have at least one sacrificial friendship.

## A NOTE FROM MAX

*Every person is in dire need of at least one faithful friend or a mate who will look them in the eye and say, "I will never leave you. You may grow old and gray, but I'll never leave you. Your face may wrinkle and your body may ruin, but I'll never leave you. The years may be cruel and the times may be hard, but I'll be here. I will never leave you."*

*Think for a minute about the people in your world. What do they think of your commitment to them? Does your loyalty ever waver? Do you have one person with whom your "contract" is nonnegotiable?*

*Once, two friends were fighting together in a war. The combat was ferocious, and many lives were being taken. When one of the two young soldiers was injured and could not get back to the trenches, the other went out to get him against his officer's orders. He returned mortally wounded, and his friend, whom he had carried back, was dead.*

*The officer looked at the dying soldier, shook his head, and said, "It wasn't worth it."*

*The young boy, overhearing the remark, smiled and said, "But it was worth it, sir, because when I got to him he said, 'Jim, I knew you'd come.'"*

*Make the most of your relationships. Follow the advice of Benjamin Franklin: "Be slow in choosing friends and be even slower in leaving them."*[2]

*Redefining* {beau · ti · ful}

Three words come to mind through David's story, and God gives us these words so we can evaluate the quality of our friendships: *loving, sacrificial, spiritual*. Use them to define what a beautiful friendship looks like.

*Loving.* Jonathan could easily have become jealous of attractive, popular, and talented David. But the Bible says Jonathan loved David as he loved himself (1 Samuel 20:17), so he put David first. Sometimes, though, we can find ourselves in competition with our friends. We may occasionally feel a twinge of jealousy when they're getting attention we'd like to have. Anytime a jealous or competitive thought enters our minds, we need to remember why our friend is our friend. Hopefully it's because we love her and we therefore should want what is best for her. That kind of love means celebrating with her the good things that happen in her life. In return, a good friend shows us that same kind of love when things are going our way. I've learned that it saves me a lot of stress and emotional trauma when I choose to be happy for my friends instead of envious.

*Sacrificial.* Sometimes in a relationship we have to give and take. Letting go of something to please a friend is a true sacrifice. In this case, Jonathan put his life on the line for David. In our lives, the sacrifice may just mean eating somewhere other than our favorite restaurant because we know our friend doesn't like it. Or it may mean giving up that movie we really wanted to see because our friend needs someone to listen to her. Sacrifices show our friend that she is a priority and that she really matters to us. And, remember, a true friend will return the favor.

*Spiritual.* When Jonathan hid David from his father's wrath, he came up with a plan for warning David if Saul chose to kill him.

While telling David the plan, he said, "Remember, the LORD is witness between you and me forever" (1 Samuel 20:23). Jonathan included God in his plan and in his relationship with David. They did not hesitate to bring up God's name when they were with each other. But are we like Jonathan and David? Does our faith flourish in our relationships? Or are we in a lot of friendships where we are afraid to talk about our faith? David and Jonathan's relationship was centered on God. On what are our friendships centered? Are they centered on gossip, boys, and fashion? Are they constant *drama*? Or are they built on things that really matter? Here's the deal: When we can talk about God in a friendship, we will find ourselves snorkeling in the deep part of the ocean. Our hearts connect on such a deep level that our relationship becomes exciting, encouraging, and meaningful. True friends love that we love God.

### Trendy Friendships

I had a friend in high school whose parents were divorced. Everyone loved her, but they joked behind her back about her being a snob. At the time, I thought she was snobby because that's who she really was. But looking back, I think I know exactly why she flaunted her designer clothes and boasted about her latest shopping spree. You see, she lived with her mom, and her dad, a very wealthy man, gave her almost everything she wanted. Maybe that was how he loved her, how he made up for his absence in her life. He bought her things. It may be, too, that her mom, feeling guilty about the divorce, made up for her daughter's pain with presents as well. Although she and I shared a degree of closeness, she betrayed me in order to obtain a trendy status with a certain group of popular girls. Since her dad loved her with money and shallow gifts, maybe she looked at friends as another trendy item that might fill her empty heart.

*What type of friend are you?*

_____

_____

_____

_____

_____

_____

_____

## Drama Trauma

God can help us girls lose the drama. Trust me, drama is not a good look. People who surround themselves with or create drama do not strike others as beautiful. They mostly strike others as annoying. I know this because I've seen these annoying people, and I've been one of these annoying people.

God longs to see us in friendships that encourage us to be our best spiritually and emotionally and that teach us not only how to love selflessly and sacrificially but also how to be loved. If our friendships don't have those qualities, let's stop and ask ourselves why. Maybe God is nudging us to find friends we can be ourselves around. Maybe God is asking us to step it up as a friend. Maybe we need to dive deeper in our healthy, but shallow, relationships. Let's be sure to listen to what our Dad wants to tell us. He cares! And if we let him, he will fill our lives with emotionally healthy and uplifting relationships and leave the drama for reality television.

## LIFE ACCESSORY
### Peace—in believing God is in control

Okay, you want me to tell you a big secret of mine? I love drama! I do! I think it's complex, exciting, and interesting to solve. Why do you think TV is so appealing? It's show after show of drama! Drama makes for a good story, and I love a good story. Deep down, though we say we hate it, there is usually a little naughty side of us that loves a big slice of drama. So what does God think about drama? It's not like there is a verse that says, "Thou shalt not be a drama mama." But he does say that drama only leads to a destructive life. If you want a long and healthy life, seek peace. "Whoever would love life and see good days must keep his tongue from evil and his lips from deceitful speech. He must turn from evil and do good; he must seek peace and pursue it." (I Peter 3:10–11). Drama may be momentarily interesting, but peace is what will be remembered.

God wants to be the Dad we run to when our friendships stress us out. Maybe this would be a good time to take what we have talked about and ask God to help us look at our friendships the way he wants us to look at them.

*Father, I ask you to help me be a good friend to others. Give me wisdom in choosing friends who will encourage me and love me for who I really am. Give me a fresh outlook on what my relationships with others should be like. I ask that my friendships be centered on you. Amen.*

chapter twelve

{ people who
are breathing }

*T*rue beauty doesn't just show up when we want it to. It's not just there to help us catch Prince Charming or to benefit our friendships. God has made us beautiful for a lot of reasons. And we need to display that beauty for . . . well . . . for people who are breathing. And that pretty much covers everyone.

But, before you start rolling your eyes, wondering why you need to respect your drill sergeant principal or be kind to the weird kid who writes poems about you, here are just a few reasons it's in our best interest to let our beauty shine:

> •*It brings glory to God.*

> •*It brings joy to others.*

> •*It brings endless blessings to our own lives.*

Earlier we talked about my friend Hannah's dad and how he didn't complain about his bosses and always showed respect. So why does that even matter?

## Hannah's Story

Ask Hannah what her passion was in high school, and without any hesitation, she will boldly broadcast that volleyball was her life. She read books about it. She arrived early and stayed late at practice. She even dreamed about volleyball! But she told me that more important than learning to serve a floater or approach an outside hit was what her relationship with her volleyball coach taught her about why respecting authority is a key to success.

You see, Hannah hadn't always listened to her coach. She hadn't always thought this whole "obey your leaders" thing was *that* important. Here is her story:

*During the summer before tenth grade, my driving goal was to make varsity as a sophomore. That passion burned so strong within me that it was all I could think about. During those summer months, my coach encouraged me to join the varsity team at the summer camps they attended. I did well competing against the older girls, and when our seasonal practices started, I thought for sure my name would be on the varsity list.*

*One Friday, midway through our last two-a-day practice, the coach posted the JV and varsity teams. My eyes quickly*

scrolled through the varsity list . . . "Hannah Crosby . . .
Hannah Crosby . . . Where is Hannah Crosby?" Sure enough,
to my devastation, I found my name on the JV list.

I was instantly angry and offended! Hiccupping back
tears of rage, I stormed off the court and hid in a hallway. I
sat there stewing over my "idiot coaches" who had done this
to me, and I considered quitting altogether. Eventually, a
teammate found me and dragged me back into practice. For
the rest of practice, I was lazy, selfish, and rude. It's embarrassing to remember my attitude now that I look back on that
day! It was as if I thought I could change my coach's mind
by being disrespectful!

That weekend I spent a lot of time alone in my room
thinking about where I'd gone wrong. The summer camps
seemed to have gone so well. Slowly, I began to recall several
times over the previous few months when my coaches had
given me specific instructions on my skills or footwork, and I
knew in my heart that I had not followed their coaching. I
had neglected to listen to any of their advice. I had a major
pride problem, and it was influencing the way I reacted to
their authority. It hit me like a ton of bricks, and I wished I
could redo the previous three months of my life. Since I
couldn't change the past, I would change the future, and from
then on I was a different player.

I went early to practice and stayed late in order to get
more repetitions in. I read sports psychology books, and I
even loved the part of practice everyone else hated . . . condi-
tioning. More than anything, I craved any attention I could
get from the authority figure in my life who could help me the

most: *my coach. When he spoke, I listened. When he said run, I sprinted. I trusted him to help me accomplish my goals. My definition of authority began to change. I finally understood that if I obeyed my coach, then I would excel because he knew the most about the game.*

*Generally, the word* authority *had always meant rules, guidelines, and consequences. But in this new light, authority meant opportunity, wisdom, and triumph. I wanted authority—I needed authority—to help me be my best self! By midseason, my coaches were delighted in the change they saw in me and decided to have me split time between JV and varsity. By my junior year, I was a starter on varsity, and I was captain of the team my senior year.*

*I attribute my ability to learn these lessons to my dad. He has taught me to have a solid work ethic and to accept responsibility. Most importantly, he has taught me that our attitudes and actions toward authority are a reflection of how we respond to the authority of God. I have learned that when we respect authority, some of that respect flows back to us from others. Good things come back—rewards! And I see this truth every day in the respect people show my dad.*

## Gold Medals and Madonna

Because of her dad, Hannah's entire understanding of authority changed. Instead of blowing off instruction, she recognized the benefits that come from listening to and following advice. If you don't have a good example of respect in your house, then let God teach you how to act around adults and leaders.

Check out these verses below to see how God wants us to act around adults.

*Submit yourselves for the Lord's sake to every authority insti-*
*tuted among men. —1 Peter 2:13*

*Submit yourselves to your masters with all respect, not only*
*to those who are good and considerate, but also to those who*
*are harsh. For it is commendable if a man bears up under the*
*pain of unjust suffering because he is conscious of God. —1*
*Peter 2:18—19*

After reading those verses, you might react the way I did when I first read them: *Why would God want us to respect a man or woman who is harsh or unjust? That's not fair!*

A couple of years ago I had the privilege of working with Laura Wilkinson, an Olympic diver. Representing the USA at the 2000 games in Sydney, Laura won a gold medal for her plat-form dives. But I can't talk about Laura without mentioning her heart for Jesus. She dives for him every time. During the 2008 Beijing Olympics, one announcer after another commented on her impressive character. I've always giggled at the thought of hanging out at the neighborhood pool with Laura and watching kid after kid do cannonball after cannonball . . . until Laura walks up to the diving board.

Try to get in my head with me (I know that's a scary thought). Imagine being with Laura and me at the neighborhood pool on a hot summer day. We beg Laura to show us that twisty, flippy spin dive (I don't think that's its technical name) that we watched her do on TV. After much pestering, she gives in. But as she walks toward the high dive, the lifeguard stops her.

"I'm sorry, ma'am, but that high dive is reserved for our swim team. They have been properly trained to use a high dive. You'll have to use the standard diving board."

"No, you don't understand," she replies. "I *am* properly trained. I'm an Olympic diver."

"Yeah, and I'm Madonna," the lifeguard says with a sarcastic tone of disbelief.

Can you imagine Laura's frustration? If only the lifeguard knew who she was! There he is, telling an Olympic diver that she is not properly trained to use the high dive! The nerve! But what a humbling scenario.

Has anyone ever underestimated your talents? It's humbling. I can't think of anyone who has been more underestimated than God. And he faced it with beautiful humility. Imagine going from a life in heaven, where everything is glorious, peaceful, and beautiful, to living on earth with sweaty armpits, aching joints, and grumpy people! Jesus went from creating the kings who were in power to obeying them. He understood humility more completely than we ever will. He went from being *the* authority to serving authority. His example can definitely reshape our outlook on obedience and respect.

If God himself respected authority on earth, then you and I must do so too—and compared to what Jesus was called to do, we have it easy when it comes to submitting. One of the greatest qualities that God rewards is humility, and if anyone knows anything about humility, it's Jesus.

## A NOTE FROM MAX

*You know the coolest thing about the coming of Christ? You know the most remarkable part of Jesus' time on earth?*

*Not just that he swapped eternity for calendars.*

*Not that the One who played marbles with the stars gave it up to play marbles with marbles.*

*Not that he, in an instant, went from needing nothing to needing air, food, a tub of hot water and salts for his tired feet, and, more than anything, needing somebody—anybody—who was more concerned about where he would spend eternity than where he would spend Friday's paycheck.*

*Not that he refused to defend himself when blamed for every sin of every person who ever lived.*

*Not even that after three days in a dark hole he stepped into the Easter sunrise with a smile and a swagger and a question for lowly Lucifer—"Is that your best punch?"*

*That was cool, incredibly cool.*

*But want to know the coolest thing about the One who gave up the crown of heaven for a crown of thorns?*

*He did it for you. Just for you.*[1]

So, because of what Christ has done for us and through us, he can offer us grace to show toward the difficult teacher, the whiny neighbor, or even the snotty lifeguard. But what about people a little closer to home? Or in some cases, *in* our home? The fam. You know, the people with our DNA.

Siblings are annoying. There. I said it.

Sometimes it's just hard to love your sisters and brothers, isn't it? I grew up with two younger sisters, so I can't relate to you girls with brothers, but let me just say how much I deeply respect you.

I do know a lot, though, about how sisters can fight. There were two areas my sisters and I fought about the most: shotgun (not the weapon, so don't freak out) and closets. We fought so much over who got to sit in the front seat going to school that Dad had to make up a rule: Andrea sat up front on odd days, and I sat up front on even days. We also had closet catastrophes on a weekly basis. If Andrea took a shirt out of my closet without asking me, you'd have thought from my reaction that she'd borrowed one of my legs! How dare she touch my prized possessions! (I love how Mom bought me everything, yet I claimed it all as "mine.")

Do you fight a lot with your siblings, or do you get along pretty well? Struggling with siblings from time to time is normal. But if the relationship is more like a never-ending rivalry, stop and ask yourself why. What can you do to change that?

I know that respecting family members can sometimes seem like an impossible task, but this truth might help us: we need to remember that our heavenly Dad is the Dad of our siblings and parents too. So when you're ready to pull your sister's hair out by the roots and kick your brother in the shin, think about this:

*Whoever wants to become great among you must be your servant, and whoever wants to be first must be your slave—just as the Son of Man did not come to be served, but to serve, and to give his life as a ransom for many. —Matthew 20:26–28*

We all want to be great, don't we? Well, what does this verse say we have to do in order to become great? We have to act humbly! We have to serve!

God wants us to look at our family and at all the adults in our life (yes, even the mean ones) with humble eyes. He wants us to see those relationships as a chance to love others just as he loves us. So if that means apologizing to your brother or sister before he or she apologizes to you, try it. If that means walking out of the room before you blow up at your mom again, respectfully walk out.

*Think about some other ways you can show humility at home, and then write them down here:*

_____

_____

_____

_____

_____

_____

Redefining {beau·ti·ful}

*Being beautiful means overflowing in love for others. It's not always easy, but who said life was easy? Besides, what does that say about our character if we can only be nice to people who are nice to us?*

*God fills us with his love not only to show us how much he loves us but so that it will overflow to others. Sometimes wearing this accessory will come naturally, but other times it takes a bit of effort. Just to get some practice, make a point to do three kind things for three random people today. Journal about how you felt and how you might be blessed by it.*

Once we see God as our Dad, he becomes our example of how to see and deal with others. We may not see a change in other people, but they will see a change in us. So let's choose to follow God's example so that we can be an example. God will redefine our relationships, making them less dramatic (what girl doesn't want less drama in her life?), less burdensome, more joyful, and more beautiful.

*God, I ask you to guide me through relationships with my family and with the adults and other leaders in my life. I ask that I would look at them as you look at them and love them the way you love them. Amen.*

*chapter thirteen*

# { your story }

*T*his chapter is all about you, girl! We are going to take this concept of beauty and write a little story about the beauty in your own life. Wait! Don't walk away! I promise, this will not be a graded assignment, and you do not have to write it alone. We can write it together.

I just wanted to spend a little time letting you take all of the beauty tips, life accessories, and relationship chats we have had and apply them to your own life. That way, you don't have to walk away from this book thinking, *Jenna, all of that may sound great, but there is no way my life can look beautiful. There is no way that relationship with my dad or my mom or even God can look beautiful. And I don't know if I can ever see myself as beautiful.*

Even the darkest stories can have a beautiful ending. No matter what story you have had thus far, we are going to figure out a way to make it even more beautiful.

So, let's start.

Every story needs a title.

How about . . . "My Life. A Novel." No. Way too boring. How

about . . . "Extreme Heart Makeover." No, that sounds a little too familiar.

*Okay, how about you just title your story, yourself. After all, this is your story, not mine.*

---

---

---

Now that you have your title, let's think of a killer first sentence. "It was the best of times and the worst of times," has already been taken by some famous guy named Dickens, so we better go with something more simple. Hmmm . . . how about, "Once upon a time"? It may be unoriginal, but it always works! Plus, what girl doesn't like a story where she is a princess? And every princess story has "once upon a time." So here we go:

*Once upon a time there was a princess named _____ who lived in a huge castle (the castle part may be a little exaggerated) in _____.*

Okay, now let's break down the kind of family situation you were born into. Take the lines below and write about your parents.

*Were they together? Do you know both of your parents? Were you adopted? Were they divorced? Then, talk about how many siblings*

*Redefining* {beau·ti·ful}

*you have and where you fall in line on the age train. Are you the oldest? youngest? middle?*

_____

_____

_____

_____

_____

_____

_____

_____

_____

_____

    All right, so you know how we've been talking about how your dad is the primary figure that affects how beautiful we are inside and out? Well, write a little bit about your earthly dad. Sorry there isn't much room, but feel free to use the margins or the back of the cover. If you don't like to write, you can draw a picture. Hey, it's your story! Do what you want. Here are some topics to consider:

*Where does your dad work? Is he married, single, or dating? What are his hobbies? What kind of dad is he? What sort of relationship do you have with him?*

_____

_____

_____

_____

We also decided that all earthly dads mess up, right? Sometimes their mess ups make things pretty ugly. They can't save you from the craziness of life. This is the part of the story where we need to discuss a problem. Every story has a problem. The problem in your story needs to answer this question: *What in your life has prevented you from having beautiful relationships and having a beautiful perception of yourself?* It may be that this is where you want to get honest about the hurt your dad or mom has caused. It may be that you want to focus more on the lies of your peers or the media. It also may be that you want to focus on yourself and bad habits that you have formed, whether it is an addiction or selfishness, harbored bitterness or lack of gratitude.

*What are some of the problems that keep you from experiencing the beautiful life God wants to give you and experiencing the beautiful self God has called you to be?*

_____

_____

_____

_____

Because you are getting vulnerable, I'll get vulnerable. A problem in my story was the insecurity I had because of my dad's success. I thought I'd always be known as "Max Lucado's daughter" and never just as "Jenna." So I created all these false expectations for myself; I felt I had to be the perfect and successful daughter that I thought everyone expected me to be. It took me a long time to understand that my identity doesn't come from his success or even my own.

Because of the problem in our stories, we make bad decisions: we have unhealthy relationships. My cousin Holly knows what it is like to suffer in the problem of her life story.

**Holly's Story**

She was eight years old when she heard words that changed her life forever: "We are getting a divorce." She told me that she felt like a Ping-Pong ball growing up, bouncing from one house to the next. She even ran away from home because she didn't want to pack her bags one more time. She longed for stability but felt confused; she longed for family unity but grew up having to choose between two battling parents; and she longed for a daddy's love, but he lived somewhere else.

When she was older, Holly got honest about how her dad's decision to cheat on her mom defined so many areas in her life. For instance, she fought with her brother because he would take their dad's side while she took their mom's. It was also difficult for her to trust men because the primary man in her life had betrayed her mom. And the divorce made her angry with God. She questioned why he would let this happen.

*Take a minute to list a few of the areas where the problems in your life story have hurt your outlook or the relationships in your life.*

_____

_____

_____

_____

Some of you may not want to continue the story after that section. After looking at the problems in your life, you may want to throw this book across the room. You don't know how anything beautiful can come from this. Whatever you're thinking, don't lose hope. I've got good news! You don't have to write the rest of your story! Remember when we were hanging out a handful of chapters ago, and we started talking about your heavenly Dad? Well, he happens to be a best-selling Author who specializes in happy endings. He is here to write the rest of your story. I've invited him to come and help you, but he told me that my invite can only do so much. He needs *you* to invite him.

God longs to take the ashes from your life and turn them into beauty (Isaiah 61:3). He wants to help you embrace your story and grow from it. The only way you can do that is by letting him have the master pen. With God writing your story, I can guarantee your life on earth won't turn out exactly as you planned, but there is no doubt you will have a heavenly "happily ever after."

## A NOTE FROM MAX

*There is more to your life than you ever thought. There is more to your story than what you have read. There is more to your song than what you have sung. A good author saves the best for last. A great composer keeps his finest for the finish. And God, the author of life and composer of hope, has done the same for you.*

> *The best is yet to be.*
> *And so I urge you, don't give up.*
> *And so I plead, finish the journey.*
> *And so I exhort, be there.*
> *Be there when God whispers your name.*[1]

If you already see beauty in your relationships and in yourself, God wants to make your story even more beautiful. Don't count yourself out of this!

So how does God create beautiful endings? First, he waits for us to hand him the pen and then to ask him to change the way our story is going. When we invite God to be our first and most important Dad, he edits the way we look at our problems. He edits the way we act in our relationships, the way we think of ourselves, and the way we think of him. He makes our story beautiful.

Are you ready to turn the writing over to the One who wants to write your story? If so, great. If not, ask God to help you. This would be a perfect time to ask him to take over your heart as well. Spend a minute with God, asking him to take control over your heart and your story.

So how does God write a beautiful ending? He uses the problems in your story to make *you* a stronger *you*! He uses the problems in your story by putting people in your life going through the same struggles. And he uses the problems in your story to grow you closer to him. Check out the rest of Holly's story to see what I'm talking about:

## A BEAUTIFUL ENDING

Holly said that her story turned a new page when she turned to God. She explained that God and her church family helped her forgive her dad, a step that freed her from anger and resentment. She became a part of a class her church offered for children going through divorce. This class offered her a lot of encouragement, and she is now active in helping other children going through what she went through. She began a new and stronger relationship with her dad, because she had fallen in love with her perfect Dad. She also found the man of her dreams and has been happily married for about six years now.

Maybe the problem in your story is so dismal that you can't even write about it, let alone see light at the end of this dark journey. If so, you may relate to this story:

## Joyce's Story

Joyce Meyer shares her story in her book *Beauty for Ashes*. Joyce grew up with a dad who sexually abused her the entire time she lived at home. When she tried to tell her mom, her mom chose to believe her dad, who claimed that Joyce was lying. Joyce remembers how her entire body filled with fear whenever she heard his key turning the lock at night.[2] Fear dominated her life, and this fear was so paralyzing that she didn't even know how to make friends.

Joyce felt stuck for a long time. She remained in the pit of despair for years until she started feasting on God's Word and finally handed over the pen, letting God be the Author of the rest of her story. But how could he transform her tragedy into triumph?

Well, Joyce says in her book that she had to face the truth about herself before she could move on with her life.[3] For Joyce, facing the truth meant acknowledging the bad attitude she had toward the world because of the unhealed pain from her past.

What truth about yourself do you need to face?

*Maybe your dad is abusive. Maybe he's wonderful. Regardless of your story, everyone has secret insecurities. When your inside hurts, it shows on the outside in the way you act, in the way you dress, in the way you sleep at night. Here are just some ideas based on Joyce's story that might help your inside become beautiful so your outside can be beautiful:*

- *Face the fact that you have been hurt. You keep shrugging off the pain, but the more you shrug, the more you run. And running away from a problem will not resolve it.*

- *Examine your symptoms. Do you stay in bed a lot or isolate yourself a lot? Do you feel sad all the time, or is your world always gray? Do you fight a lot with friends or family? These are all symptoms of a heart that is suppressed or even depressed.*

- *Face your hatred toward your dad, hatred toward yourself, or your hatred toward whoever has hurt you. Or—and here's a big one—what if it's time that you get honest about your anger toward God?*

See, until you and I look at what is going on in our hearts, we won't hand God the pen to write a story of healing and redemption. We won't know how to fully love.

Another truth Joyce faced was the harsh past her own father had experienced growing up. He himself had suffered abuse, so he didn't know what healthy parenting looked like. Did it excuse his behavior? No! But did it give her compassion? Yes. Have you looked at the story behind the scenes in your problem? Have you talked to the person who hurts you about his or her past? Is that unhealthy relationship in your life due to a broken home life?

Okay, so here is my challenge. Go back to the section where you wrote down problems and how they have affected different parts of your life. Now I want you to write a prayer to God, asking him to use each of the problems in a specific way, turning them into something beautiful. Here's my example from my own life:

*God, I struggle with being my true self because of a lot of friends who have betrayed me in the past, a lot of friends who didn't like me for me. Will you use that as a way for me to depend on you for my self-worth and identity? Will you use it as a reminder for me to encourage my friends in their uniqueness?*

## LIFE ACCESSORY
### Joy—in knowing the Source of all joy

*Joyce found joy in her story. She now speaks to thousands of women every year about God and his faithfulness in her life. She has written countless books and used her experience to bring joy to others who are stuck in the problem part of their life stories. Another joy was found in her passion for God's Word.*

*In God's Word you will find all the tools you need to mend broken relationships, mend your own heart, and live a life that is full of joy! But here's the catch: you can't just read the Bible; you have to live it. The Bible says, "Faith without good deeds is useless" (James 2:20 NLT).*

> *True joy comes from living out the beautiful life that God calls you to in his Word. So try it out! Print out verses that will help you forgive more, love more, and serve more. You can even cut out the verses I have given you in this book! It may not start out easy, but I promise, joy will swallow up any dark pit the more you cling to Jesus and his words of life.*

If your life has, overall, been a smooth ride, remember God wants to use your positive experience to shape you. And he wants to use your knowledge of what a good dad looks like, what healthy relationships and strong self-esteem look like to help girls who have never known a positive role model. Maybe after reading this chapter, you are looking at that mean girl at school a little differently. Now you may be wondering if she has a good home and if she knows she has a perfect Dad who loves her. Maybe God wants you to reach out to someone because of what you've learned.

How do you want your story to end? Do you want to remain bitter, apathetic, wounded, angry, or depressed? Or do you want to let God redefine your life and discover health, joy, and peace? It's time to hand him the pen so he can make your life beautiful.

*chapter fourteen*

# { perfect promise }

When I was in seventh grade, my dad gave my sisters and me a priceless Valentine's Day gift that I will never forget. He typed out a letter that he printed on three pieces of paper and put in three frames, one for each one of us. They were waiting on the kitchen table when we came bouncing downstairs, giddy with thoughts of chocolates, flowers, heart-shaped balloons, and cute teddy bears. Imagine the quizzical looks on our faces when we each received a framed letter as our gift. What I didn't understand at the time was that this piece of paper would mean more than flowers that would soon fade. The words on that paper helped shape who I am.

The letter was a promise, and I'm not talking about a promise to "tell the whole truth and nothing but the truth, so help me God." It wasn't a promise from Dad to never make a mistake, and it wasn't a promise from him to buy us anything we wanted or to let us watch the coveted PG-13 movies that all of our friends could watch. No. It was better than all of that.

It was my dad's promise to never leave us. It was his promise to love us, to provide for us, to remain faithful to our mom, and to remain faithful as a father. It was his promise to always honor our mom and always protect us.

As a middle school kid, though, how was I supposed to understand the significance of this gift? Though consciously I didn't feel any changes in my heart because of the gift, I now know that, deep down in the recesses of my soul, that promise helped grow me into a girl who trusts God, who knows how to love, who is secure in my parents' love, who knows what commitment and dedication look like, who has hope, who believes in dreams coming true, and, most of all, who knows why God wants to be called "Father."

A true father loves, forgives, never leaves, consoles, listens, helps, disciplines, and encourages. And the promise that Dad gave me that Valentine's Day morning helped teach me what this true love looks like.

You have a Dad who makes the same promise to you. You have a Dad who is defined by love (see 1 John 4:8). He holds you through long, dark nights, and he rejoices with you during happy days. He delights in you when you don't delight in yourself, and he forgives you when you can't forgive yourself. He provides everything you could ever need and gives you advice to guide your way.

So, before we say good-bye, I wanted to share a portion of the promise my dad gave to me. Read it as a letter from your perfect Dad to you, his beloved daughter. Soak in each word, because he has made these same promises to you; he has said, "Never will I leave you; never will I forsake you" (Hebrews 13:5).

*Redefining* {beau·ti·ful}

Dear _____, [Insert your name]

    *I have a special gift for you. My gift is warmth at night and sunlit afternoons, chuckles and giggles and happy Saturdays. When it's stormy out there, I want you to be safe with me. This is what I want to give you.*

    *But how do I give this gift? Is there a store that sells laughter or a catalog that offers kisses? No. Such a treasure can't be bought. But it can be given. And here is how I give it to you.*

    *Your gift is a promise: it's the promise that I will always love you. I will never leave you. You'll never wake up to find me gone. You'll never find that I have run away. You'll always have me as your Dad. And I will always cherish you as my daughter.*

    *That is my promise.*

    *That is my gift.*

> *Love,*
> *Your heavenly Daddy*

After reading this, you may want to do what my dad did for me: cut out the promise (that's right, I'm giving you permission to cut up this book) and frame it. That way, every day, you will remember your perfect Dad who will always love you, no matter what.

Well, it's been a fun makeover. We've talked about a lot of ways to change our look, and I've loved hanging out with you! Maybe one day our paths will cross again, but until then, my challenge to you is this:

Get to know God as your Dad. As you do so, he will redefine

your relationships and make them loving, God-centered, drama free, and encouraging. He will redefine the way you see yourself and make you more confident, more joyful, and more God-honoring. He will redefine the way you look at him and give you an understanding of who he really is—a perfect Father who will never leave you, who will always love you, and who wants to grow you into the woman he made you to be. Overall, your entire life becomes more beautiful when you know what God sees when God sees you.

# { acknowledgments }

*T*his book was a team effort! To everyone who had a hand in making this book possible, thank you, thank you, thank you! Here are some of the names that carried me through this experience:

**MacKenzie Howard**—I would not want to work with me as much as you had to! But because you are the perfect combination of intelligence, creativity, humility, and kindness, you learned how to put up with me. To me, you have become more than a phenomenal editor; you have become my new friend.

**Laura Minchew**—You are way too big of a deal; yet, you still took the time to edit this first-time author's elementary material. Thanks for your wisdom. Thanks for your support. Thanks for your patience. And thanks for not being too cool to help little 'ol me.

**Greg Jackson and Mandi Cofer**—Greg, I don't think the old line "Don't judge a book by its cover" applies to you because of your incredible artistic ability to make a book come to life on the outside! Mandi, I tip my hat to you—master of taking text and transforming it into art. Great job, guys!

**Mary Graham**—I would never have written this book if you hadn't asked me. Thank you for believing in me. I want to be just like you when I grow up.

**Amy Chandy**—At first you intimidated me, but now you amaze me. You don't stop with the dreaming. You stop once the dreams come true. Thank you for making one of my dreams come true by letting me be a part of the best team in the world. I admire you, Amy!

**Mom**—Thanks for crying with me when I cry and laughing with me when I laugh. No matter what I am going through, you find a way to empathize with the craziness going on in my head. You always have wisdom to impart and a hug to give. I love you.

**Andrea and Sara**—You are half of this book! Sharing a life with you inspired my stories, and you inspire me still. Dre, you inspire me to love people, live adventurously, and ask thousands of questions. Sara, you inspire me to see with spiritual eyes, laugh loud, and talk less. I love you both madly.

**Brett**—You were my biggest distraction. I caught my mind daydreaming of you when I should have been cranking out chapters! As soon as I gave you my hand, you held it tight through the ups and downs of this book. You are my closest friend, my one true love, and my rocking-chair companion. You are my favorite.

In closing, I'd like to thank all of the girls who shared their stories with me. You are the voice of this book. Without your transparency, this book would not exist. Continue to use your stories. It's the best way to make them something beautiful.

{ notes }

Chapter 3

1. Kyle Pruett, *Father Need* (New York: The Free Press, 2000), 45.
2. *Father Facts*. 5th ed. (Gaithersburg, MD: National Fatherhood Initiative, 2007), 136.
3. Kevin Leman, *What a Difference a Daddy Makes* (Nashville: Thomas Nelson, 2000), 7.
4. David Blakenhorn, "Fatherless America." Available at http://www.americanexperiment.org/publications/1993/19930113blankenhorn.php, January 13, 1993.
5. David Popenoe, *Life Without Father* (Cambridge, MA: Harvard University, 1996), 149.
6. Ibid., 143.
7. Monique Robinson, *Longing for Daddy* (Colorado Springs: WaterBrook, 2004), 120.
8. Popenoe, *Life Without Father*, 143.
9. *Father Facts*, 71.
10. Ibid., 69.
11. Pruett, *Father Need*, 38.
12. Robinson, *Longing for Daddy*, 41.
13. Leman, *What a Difference a Daddy Makes*, 159.

## Chapter 4

1. Ivy Sellers, Q&A: Dr. Meg Meeker on "Strong Fathers, Strong Daughters," Human Events, 2006. Available online at http://www.humanevents.com/article.php?id=17444.
2. Max Lucado, God's Inspirational Promises (Nashville: Thomas Nelson, 2001, 1996), 93.
3. Joyce Meyer, Beauty for Ashes (New York: Faith Words, 1994), 174.
4. Max Lucado, God Came Near: Chronicles of the Christ (Nashville: Thomas Nelson, 1986), 93–94.

## Chapter 5

1. Max Lucado, When God Whispers Your Name (Nashville: Thomas Nelson, 1994), 103.
2. Lucado, When God Whispers Your Name, 98–104.

## Chapter 6

1. Lucado, When God Whispers Your Name, 121.
2. Lucado, In the Grip of Grace (Nashville: Thomas Nelson, 1996), 171–72.
3. Lucado, The Great House of God (Nashville: Thomas Nelson, 1994), 15.

## Chapter 7

1. Max Lucado, And the Angels Were Silent (Nashville: Thomas Nelson, 1992), 58–59.

## Chapter 8

1. Nancy DeMoss, Lies Women Believe (Chicago: Moody, 2001), 68.
2. Ibid.

3. Adapted from Max Lucado, *No Wonder They Call Him the Savior* (Nashville: Thomas Nelson, 1986), 18.

Chapter 9
1. Adapted from Max Lucado, *Just Like Jesus* (Nashville: Thomas Nelson, 1995), 3.

Chapter 10
1. Chad Eastham, *The Truth About Guys* (Nashville: Thomas Nelson, 2006), 122.
2. Adapted from Max Lucado, *The Applause of Heaven* (Nashville: Thomas Nelson, 1996), 61–62.

Chapter 11
1. Max Lucado, *A Love Worth Giving: Living in the Overflow of God's Love* (Nashville: Thomas Nelson, 2002), 7.
2. Max Lucado, *On the Anvil* (Wheaton, IL: Tyndale, 1985), 127.

Chapter 12
1. Adapted from Max Lucado, *He Chose the Nails: What God Did to Win Your Heart*, electronic ed. (Nashville: Word, 2001, 2000), 23–27.

Chapter 13:
1. Max Lucado, *When God Whispers Your Name*, 192.
2. Meyer, *Beauty for Ashes*, 13.
3. Ibid., 80.